SHUT THAT DOOR!

SHUT THAT DOOR!

The Definitive Biography of Larry Grayson

Tony Nicholson

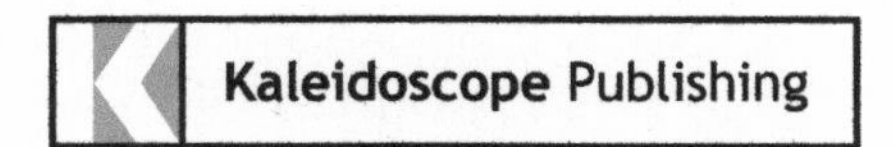

First published in hardback in Great Britain in 2017 by
Kaleidoscope Publishing
42 Victoriana Way
Handsworth Wood
B20 2SZ
United Kingdom

ISBN-13 978-1-900203-64-7

Book and cover design by Simon Coward

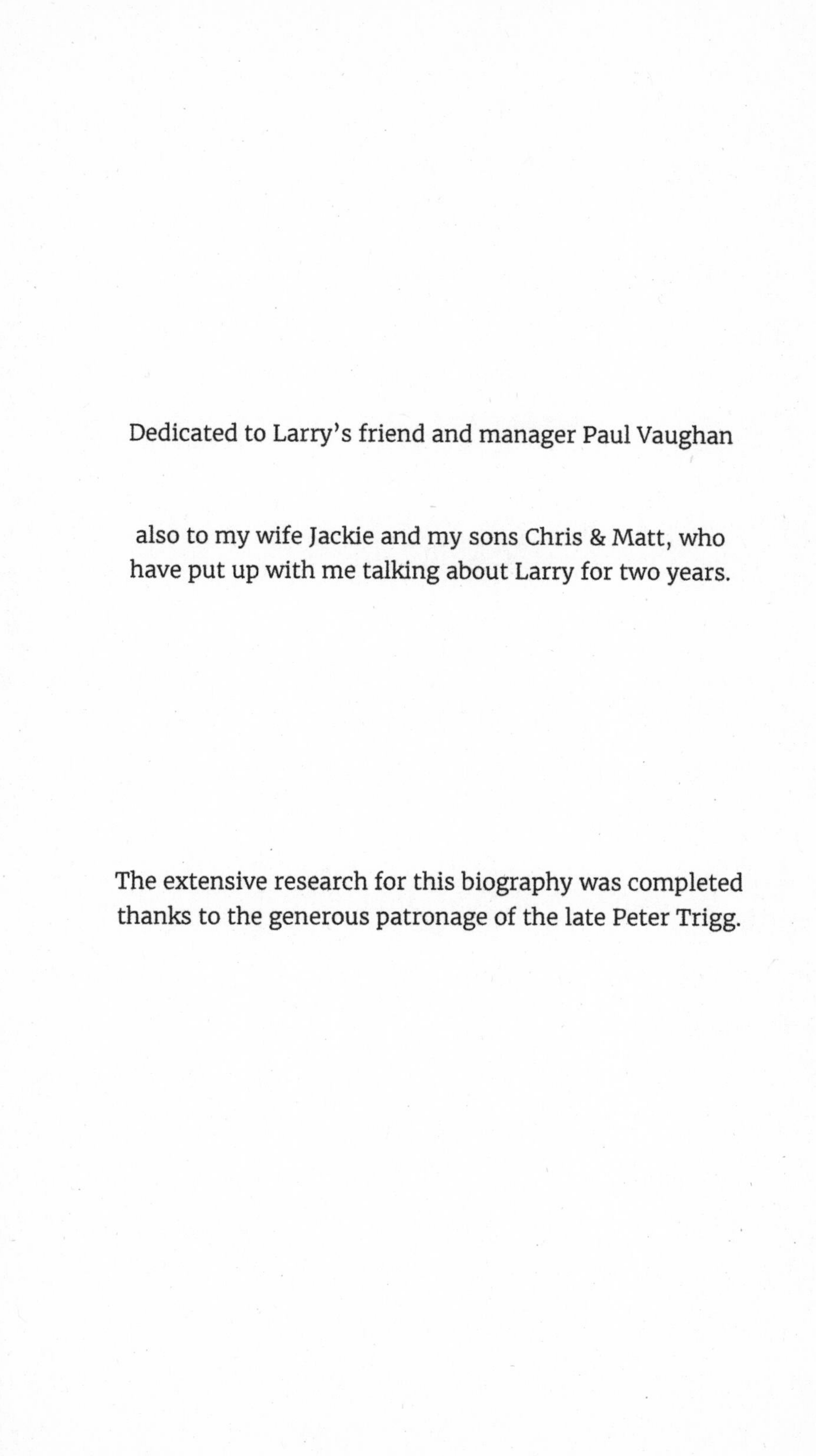

Dedicated to Larry's friend and manager Paul Vaughan

also to my wife Jackie and my sons Chris & Matt, who have put up with me talking about Larry for two years.

The extensive research for this biography was completed thanks to the generous patronage of the late Peter Trigg.

Contents

Photo Acknowledgements

The majority of photographs and illustrations come from Larry's personal collection, courtesy of Paul Vaughan, on behalf of The Larry Grayson Estate. Many were earmarked for his never-published autobiography.

Other photographs were provided by Reverend Dr Rob Marshall, Tony Chalchonowicz, or have come from the author's own collection.

Every reasonable effort has been made to trace the present copyright holders, but Kaleidoscope Publishing will be pleased to correct any errors or omissions in any future edition of this book.

Foreword by Julian Clary

I have longed to know more about the life and times of the wonderful Larry Grayson and here, at last, is a book to fill in all those gaps. Tony Nicholson's *Shut That Door* is a very thorough and meticulous account of Grayson's life and career and a fair and candid look at his private life, such as it was.

Written with affection and sensitivity, this long overdue biography tells the remarkable story of how an illegitimate child born in a grim workhouse in Banbury, Oxfordshire in 1923 became one of the biggest mainstream TV stars of the 70s.

As an effeminate child of impressionable age I watched, learned and laughed at *Larry Grayson's Generation Game* each Saturday night. The catchphrases ('Seems like a nice boy,' 'Look at the muck in 'ere!' 'What a gay day!') worked their way into the Clary family's every day parlance and I waited eagerly each week to hear the latest about Larry's gallery of wayward friends Everard, Slack Alice and Apricot Lil.

Of course I didn't then realize that Grayson was carrying on a tradition of camp comedy from the likes of Music Hall legends Sid Field and Douglas Byng or that he was paving the way for me, Paul O'Grady, Graham Norton and Alan Carr in years to come.

I knew nothing of the close-knit Nuneaton community that had inspired his particular brand of comedy, or the decades he had spent honing his act on the rough and ready Midlands club circuit. I didn't (at that age) register the gay references or appreciate the fine line he was treading or the brilliance of his timing. I only knew that he was the funniest man on television.

And then, just as quickly as he had burst on to our screens, it seems he went out of fashion.

In the mid-eighties, as I made my way in the world, I doubt I thought much about how Grayson influenced my own style of comedy or the debt I owe him.

But I do know that when I performed at the London Palladium in 1991 I sat in the dressing room and thought with wonder about the stars I loved and admired that had trod those very boards before me. I read in this lovely, informative book that Larry did the same in 1974. He thought of his idols Judy Garland and Gracie Fields… I'm proud to say that I thought about Larry Grayson.

Julian Clary

Introduction

If I were to tell you that this book is about Billy White, I think you'd probably find it rather interesting. Billy was an illegitimate baby, born in a bleak, grim old workhouse building in leafy Banbury in Oxfordshire. The year was 1923, a time when being born out of wedlock was definitely not the best start in life. The ugly word 'bastard' still had literal and very unkind meaning. Baby Billy's mother had no choice but to give him away to a poor but loving foster family, for fear of being ostracised by her own parents. Billy's new foster parents lived in the industrial Midlands, and his foster mother tragically died when Billy was still a little boy, leaving their youngest daughter to bring him up as her own. Billy went on to have an extraordinary life, but sadly died before his time, rather lonely and unloved, still with firmly held beliefs in God, guardian angels, clairvoyants and Red Indian spirit guides. When I tell you that Billy White changed his name to Larry Grayson and, along the way, became one of our best loved entertainers, I think you'll find this book absolutely fascinating.

Sadly, just before Larry's death, the showbusiness tide had turned. Ruthless television executives were suddenly turning their backs on mainstream entertainment, which seemed disingenuous as it had made them all so much money for decades. Variety performers, even showbiz legends, were suddenly being overlooked, and worse still derided. At the same time militant gay rights groups had begun loudly insisting that overtly camp performances were considered to be politically incorrect. Had performers like Larry Grayson and John Inman been straight comedians lampooning gay men, I could have sympathised with their outrage, but as both men were pretty much the same on-screen and off, it seemed ironically almost homophobic to attempt to ban them from being themselves.

Rightly or wrongly Larry Grayson had become unfashionable, and therefore virtually unemployable. Sadly, if he had just lived a little longer, he would have almost certainly come out of the other side of that showbiz trough to be reborn as a national treasure, which is precisely what happened to veteran mainstream entertainers like Frankie Howerd, Bob Monkhouse, Bruce Forsyth and Ken Dodd. He would have also lived to see gay comedians getting away with being as camp as they wanted to be, without being lambasted by militant gay activists. Larry undoubtedly paved the way for the likes of Julian Clary, Paul O'Grady, Alan Carr and Graham Norton.

Prior to that lamentable period in British showbusiness history, during which mainstream stars were shunned and cast aside, Larry Grayson had been at the very top: one of the most successful and popular British entertainers of his time... and he loved every minute of it...

Larry used to close every show with the words "I love you very much!" It may sound like a sentimental showbusiness platitude, but he sincerely meant it. There were really only ever three real loves in his adult life: his 'sister' Fan, more of her later; his dogs; and us, his public. Larry genuinely adored his audience. When we cheered and applauded him at the end of a show, that outpouring of love from his fans filled him with emotion and he reciprocated in an often choked voice: "Goodnight, God bless and... I love you very much!"

In my capacity as a television producer, working predominantly in the field of entertainment, I have been privileged, and I use that word advisedly, to meet and spend quality time with some of the funniest people in Britain. One of those, I'm delighted to say, was Larry Grayson. I made a series of twenty programmes with him for BBC1, back in the late 1980s. My first job was to take him and his manager Paul Vaughan out to lunch, to convince them that the programme was right for Larry. Two things have always stuck with me about that lunch, and bear in mind I'd never met Larry before. Firstly it was the funniest meal I have ever had in my entire life, and actually probably the longest. I laughed until the tears rolled into my soup, and I ended up pushing my plate away for fear of asphyxiating on my main course. We had sat down soberly and all business-like at twelve noon, and three giggling inebriates were politely but firmly asked to leave the quaintly posh Birmingham hotel dining room at five o'clock because they needed to clear the tables for dinner.

My second abiding memory is the parting that day. Larry thanked me sincerely and most profusely for being such a good audience. I couldn't believe it. I tried to assure him that the pleasure had all been mine, and I wanted to thank him for the most hilarious lunch I'd ever enjoyed, but he insisted I'd been a joy to entertain. Larry could take to you, or not, quite quickly, and he and I just seemed to click. I'd swear as I watched the four of them leaving (double vision by this point!) that I heard Larry say to his manager "Seems like a nice boy!" He probably didn't quite say that, but I'd like to think that he did. Whatever it was I think he was being complimentary. I liked Larry Grayson instantly.

I am honoured to be writing this definitive biography, and I owe a great debt of gratitude to Paul Vaughan, Larry's former manager, for all his enthusiastic and selfless help in pulling the book together, against all odds. The one problem with writing the life story of a deceased gay man is that there are no descendants to tap for their memories. I'll do my best. And I will also do my best to be as honest and revealing as I promise to be affectionate and eulogising with this biographical tribute to a truly great British entertainer.

Author's Note and Acknowledgements

Strangely there has never been a detailed or complete biography of Larry Grayson before now. Strange because he was such a huge star in his time. There were a couple of television documentaries made about him, and the odd biographical piece is available on the internet, but I have found them all to be woefully inaccurate. Maybe that was the problem. Nobody could find the real story.

As I write this I am collaborating on a major new ITV documentary about Larry, which promises to set the record straight and be a proper in-depth tribute to this comedy legend, and hopefully will show a whole new generation how special he was as an entertainer.

Larry did seriously think about writing an autobiography in the 1980s, and I have been privileged to have exclusive access to his comprehensive and detailed handwritten notes for that never-completed or published book. I have also had access to his own personal scrapbook – a massive and fascinating leather-bound tome which he painstakingly updated throughout his long and interesting rollercoaster of a career. You may well have heard some different interpretations of his life story, but this biography is largely based on his own personal and private recollections and memoirs, which I have to assume are more accurate than anything that has gone before.

I have also spent a couple of years doing extensive detective work, which has, at times, been frustrating as it has been hard to clarify and correct inaccurate stories and fading memories. It has been harder still because of the lack of living family and the total absence of descendants. I am satisfied however that what you are about to read is the full and truly accurate account of an entertainment legend, and a fascinating human being, with an inspirational, funny and, at times, heart-breaking story.

I am of course indebted to many of his showbusiness colleagues and friends who have generously given of their valuable time to share their personal reminiscences of the late great Larry Grayson. In no particular order I'd like to thank: Julian Clary, Michael (Lord) Grade, Alan Boyd, Marcus Plantin, Laurie Mansfield, Kevin Bishop, William G Stewart, Tony Chalchonowicz, Duggie Chapman, Keith Lascelles, Thomas Bunn, Rev Dr Rob Marshall, and especially Paul Vaughan.

I would also like to thank five friends and colleagues for their generous support and encouragement. Without them this book would have never been published: Cliff Bradley, Colin Edmonds, Chris Perry, Simon Coward, and Wendy Leavesley.

* * *

He was born William White, brought up as Billy Hammond, and, for nearly twenty years of his showbusiness career, his stage name was Billy Breen, before becoming Larry Grayson in 1956. Even after that time close friends and family still called him Bill. To simplify this confusing situation over his name, in this book I refer to him as Billy in his early years, and Larry when I am referring to him in later years, or when I am quoting things he said post-1956.

1

... an inauspicious start... but with lots of love...

In October 1974 Larry Grayson, at the age of fifty-one, was moved to tears when he saw his name and his face up in lights outside The London Palladium for the very first time. It had taken him a long time to get there. The Palladium has always been considered to be the British Mecca of variety entertainment: 'The Vatican of Showbusiness' as Larry himself called it. He'd reached the pinnacle of a remarkable career, having become a star almost overnight in his middle age. Of course like most overnight stars Larry had been grafting and perfecting his act as an unknown but nonetheless successful and seasoned entertainer for many years, around thirty-seven in Larry's case. That rather puts the 'overnight star' tag into perspective. Starring at the world-famous Palladium, taking up residence in the same Number One dressing room, previously occupied by his idols Judy Garland, Gracie Fields and Danny Kaye, must have felt like achieving the impossible for a Nuneaton lad from such humble beginnings. It was an emotional day and he rushed to a phone box to tell the one person he loved most in the world – his 'sister' Fan. This is how he recounted that conversation to his last manager, Paul Vaughan:

"Fan" Larry said, feverishly feeding in coins, "Fan. You won't believe it. I'm here in London, in a phone box, opposite the London Palladium.

"That's nice" said Fan.

"And Fan.." a wave of true emotion began to surface and his voice began to falter. "There's a huge poster, Fan, all across the theatre. It's ever so big and it's all lit up; you can't miss it. And oh Fan, my name is there above the title in the biggest letters ever. It says *'Larry Grayson, in Grayson's Scandals'*. Oh Fan!"

"Yes, well that's as maybe..." replied Fan "... but the coalman's at the door. Do we want two bags or three?"

Fan kept him grounded, but his love for her was unconditional. Their relationship was complicated. She'd quite literally been like a mother to him all his life, and she wasn't even his real sister.

William Sully White, later known to millions as comedy entertainer Larry Grayson, was born on August 31st 1923. One can hardly imagine the despair his mother, twenty-nine-year-old unmarried Ethel Rachel White, must have felt when she was forced to hand over her beloved new-born baby boy to foster parents. For a start it is hard for us to comprehend, in these more enlightened times, the stigma attached to becoming pregnant out of marriage, and subsequently giving birth to an illegitimate child. In 1923 a single mother was considered a pariah, a fallen woman. The kinder euphemism for her illegitimate offspring was 'a baby sent down from the angels'; the harsher, more judgmental word was 'bastard'. That narrow-minded mindset was presumably a legacy of Victorian Christianity, which is ironic as Christ himself was conceived out of wedlock, but that is a controversial debate for another time. The simple fact is that, back then, poor Ethel White would have been perceived as a sinner purely for being a single mother. How far things have shifted. These days a child with both parents living under the same roof is almost considered a novelty.

Larry never did meet his father and there doesn't even appear to be a reliable or definitive record of his name. However, it has been said that his father was called William Sully, which would make sense, and would obviously account for Larry's real given name. Years later Larry found out that his mother and his tall, handsome young father were very much in love when he was conceived. The unplanned pregnancy was clearly a naïve mishap – a moment of passion which got out of hand. When they got over the shock of the news Ethel's boyfriend had every intention of 'making an honest woman of her' by marrying her, and bringing the baby up together. Sadly that wasn't to be. As soon as his parents got to hear about their wedding plans all hell broke loose. The two families were of different religious persuasions, and his parents didn't want their son having any more to do with Ethel White, or her Christian Church of England family. There was to be no more talk of a wedding. The young 'courting' couple weren't even allowed to see one another ever again, and that was final. Ethel never did see her intended again, and was left to have the baby alone. It's not clear how old Larry's father was at the time, but Ethel was twenty-nine, so it seems strange now to hear of families being so strict with adult offspring and having such a final say on the matter – all in the name of their God. Larry once, with understandable bitterness, commented: "So much for religion!"

Perhaps Ethel was disappointed by the father of her unborn baby not standing up to his parents, because she rarely spoke about him ever again. She must have been heartbroken though, because it seems she never so much as looked at another man as long as she lived. When Billy / Larry got to know his mother well in later years he occasionally asked her about his father, but she never gave much away, and it was clearly a sensitive issue. He'd ask her if his dad looked like a film star – Victor Mature or Clark Gable perhaps? All Ethel would say was: "Oh, you're film mad you are!", which was true, but it didn't offer a very satisfactory answer to his question. Larry said however that she was very musical and would often sit at the piano and sing her two favourite songs: "I'll Remember You" and "He's Just My Bill". If Larry's father was indeed called William then both those titles take on a tragic poignancy. Larry always believed that Ethel still loved his absent father until the day she died.

In Larry's many attempts to unveil more about his unseen father all he discovered was that he was tall and handsome, and had married and settled down with a family at some point, presumably with somebody of a more acceptable religious faith. Ethel also once commented that Larry had his father's walk. And that's about all he ever found out.

Ethel White's parents, George and Rhoda White, lived on Blacksmith Hill in Hook Norton, a rather refined rural village near Banbury in Oxfordshire. They had a fashionably large family. Ethel was the middle child of seven siblings – two girls and five boys. Their authoritarian morally-upstanding father George was a cabinet maker, who specialised in making pianos. At a time before television, a piano was the focal point of many people's living rooms. Entertainment at home came from sing-songs around the piano, so there was plenty of demand for pianos in those days. Larry always said his real mother was a very good pianist, although she never performed professionally. For much of her adult life she made her living working 'in service', initially as a lowly housemaid, then later as a full-blown housekeeper.

Ethel's mother knew all about the pregnancy and sent her daughter away, as soon as she began to show, to have the baby at a discreet distance from home and judgmental nosy neighbours. As Larry's birthplace is recorded as Banbury in Oxfordshire, it is likely Ethel was sent to the 'home' for unmarried mothers which existed within the grim austere walls of the workhouse on Warwick Road in Banbury in those less tolerant times. Her strict Victorian father never did find out that he even had a grandson. All he knew was that Ethel had been away for a few months. Had he ever found out about the shame of her being an unmarried mother he was the sort that would have banished his own daughter with the words: "Never darken my doorstep again!", so it was very much a case of ignorance is bliss in his case. Sad though that his self-imposed rigid Christian morals robbed him of the joy of being a grandfather to little Billy White.

When her baby was born Ethel couldn't bear the thought of parting with him completely, so she refused to hand him over for adoption, which would have been the obvious course of action in those days. Instead she placed an advertisement in the local paper asking for a couple to foster her new-born. Jim and Alice Hammond from the Abbey Green area of Nuneaton were the successful applicants for the job, on the strict understanding that Ethel was to be granted regular access to see William. With a heavy heart, one cold clear November morning in 1923, Ethel White wrapped her new-born warmly in a blanket and took the train to the Trent Valley railway station in Nuneaton, where she had arranged to meet Alice Hammond and her teenage daughters May and Florence. Poor Ethel had to hand over nine-week-old baby Billy on the bustling platform, to the noisy accompaniment of shrieking whistles, belching steam, and the slamming of heavy carriage doors. One can only imagine her thoughts as she desolately stood and watched Alice's daughters push her beloved baby boy away in a brand new pram, bought by the Hammond family especially for little Billy's arrival. What a bleak journey that must have been back to Hook Norton, all alone.

Nuneaton back then was a poor but close-knit mining community, with the majority of employment being hard grimy manual labour in the powerhouse of Britain, as the industrial Midlands were known. Housing was predominantly 'two up, two down' terraces with outside lavatories, shared wash-houses, and kids playing on the cobbles in the streets. The Hammonds' home at number twenty Stanley Crescent was exactly that. Jim Hammond was a coal miner, so it was a typical working class household, with not much money, but plenty of love. A bit of extra weekly cash from Ethel for her son's upkeep may well have been part of the initial motivation for the fostering of Billy, but that didn't stop Jim and Alice showering him with love and affection, and giving him a happy and safe upbringing, which ultimately is all any of us need. The Hammonds had always wanted a boy, having already brought up two daughters of their own. The girls were now both teenagers: Mary, who preferred to use her middle name May; and her younger sister Florence, who was always referred to by the family as 'Fan', so that's what she will be called from now on in this book. Fan, who was fourteen when new-born Billy arrived into her parents' home, later recalled: "May and I had always wanted a baby brother, and then father told us that we were going to foster one. There was such excitement."

Alice Hammond had been married before to a Nuneaton coal miner called James Eatcliffe, who had died in 1916. He had suffered fatal injuries in northern France at the bloody Battle of Delville Wood during World War I. Their married name had somehow evolved into Catcliffe. Alice Catcliffe was left a widow with two young daughters – Mary Waterworth May Catcliffe, aged nine and Florence Alice Catcliffe, aged seven. Alice couldn't cope financially on her own, but she became close to a slightly older coal miner colleague and friend of her late husband, a gentle kindly man, coincidentally also called James – James Hammond. They married and Jim Hammond brought up the girls as if they were his own. They always thought of Jim as their real dad, so that is how he is referred to in this book, but of course he was actually Fan and May's step-father. It's pure supposition on my part, but it does seem likely that Jim and Alice had tried unsuccessfully to have a child of their own, which is why they decided to foster little Billy White.

At the tender young age of fourteen Fan had already left school and was out at work in a local factory, winding silk yarn off the bobbins. She clearly remembered coming home from work to hear this tiny baby squalling his head off. Her mother would be trying to quieten him before Jim came home for his supper after his arduous shift down the pit. Alice would say "He's got a good pair of lungs for such a small 'un", but Fan couldn't take her eyes off him. She later commented: "We all spoilt him from the start. He quickly became a Hammond. He was quite a beauty too, with his blonde hair and big blue eyes. He was always being photographed." Fan said that for some reason little Billy always felt extra special to her, despite the noise he made: "We all loved that little baby boy coming into our house. I knew he wasn't my real brother from the start, but that never mattered." With a loving chuckle she added: "But he was terrible at first! Crying all the time. My older sister used to say 'Oh, send him back! The child's mardy!'..." But Fan would say "Certainly not!" and scoop him up in her arms to pacify him. May was always the stricter one with Billy, whereas Fan was the soft one who always knew just how to handle this sometimes frail new addition to the Hammond family. Fan said her foster brother grew up to be a very good, caring little boy who was always happy to share everything. She always said that she couldn't remember a cross word between them, although Larry in later life said she was not averse to giving him a clip round the ear if he provoked her, even after he'd become a star in his middle age! Fan was actually quite strict in her own quiet way, not tolerating the telling of smutty jokes in her house from anybody. No matter who they were or how old they were she would firmly tell them: "We don't allow that kind of talk in this house, thank you!"

Proof, if it were needed, that handing over her new-born baby was a heartbreaking wrench for poor Ethel White came from the poignant fact that she unfailingly visited Nuneaton every week to see Billy, to bring him little gifts and longingly watch his development. She never missed, come rain or shine. Ethel had taken a live-in job in nearby Earl Shilton, so that she didn't have too far to travel. She was employed by a wealthy shop owner called Frederick Bray, one of the first people in the area to sell wireless sets (radios) and all the latest electrical innovations. Ethel worked in the shop part-time, but she was also 'in service' as Mr Bray's housekeeper in his large family home, which gave her board and lodgings. Wednesday was her half day off, so, in the afternoon, she'd hop on the bus to Nuneaton. The Hammonds would smarten Billy up, comb his hair and polish his little shoes because his 'aunty' was coming. Billy knew her as nice Aunty Ethel and became very fond of her, but he was eight years old before he discovered that adoring Aunty Ethel from Earl Shilton was in fact his mother. In later life Larry said there was never a specific formal announcement that Aunty Ethel was actually his mum. Unfortunately he learned the truth almost by osmosis from bits and pieces he picked up and overheard, especially from the wagging tongues of his gossiping school chums' mothers. In the end he asked Ethel if it was true that she was really his mum. Her confirmation didn't seem to worry him though, but he didn't want to call her 'Aunty' any more, and he felt awkward calling her mum or mother after all that time, especially as he'd always called Alice Hammond 'mum', so, from that day when he was eight, until her death in 1963, he always called his real mother 'Ethel'.

Many sources claim that Larry was adopted by Jim and Alice, but in fact that's not true. He remained Billy White all the time he was in the Hammond household, his foster home; although his schools called him Billy Hammond for simplicity's sake, and to stop awkward questions being asked. It is clear that Ethel planned right from the start that one day she would reclaim her parentage.

Larry remembered Ethel's weekly visits fondly, saying how she was always smartly dressed and nicely made up. Fortunately, despite the fifteen-year age difference, Fan and Ethel always got on well, and he recalled the tinkling of their teacups and their chit-chat as they gossiped and shared fashion tips. They'd admire each other's clothes and try on one another's hats and coats, looking at the effects in the mirror. "They both loved a bit of glamour" he said.

When Billy was old enough to behave responsibly Fan would dress him up in his best clothes, every other Saturday morning, take him on the bus to Earl Shilton, and leave him in Mr Bray's electrical shop on Wood Street with Ethel. He'd spend the whole day with his real mum, then Fan would come back to pick him up again from the rambling Bray household, after tea. Ethel clearly wanted to see as much of her son as she possibly could. She would sometimes manage to get over to Nuneaton on Sundays as well as her regular Wednesday visits.

In 1975 Larry said of Ethel White: "When I found out she was my real mother we became very close friends. She was a very gentle person. She never married. She was very quiet." Of his father Larry said: "I never really worried about my real dad. I know he got married and had a family, but he's dead now."

In the same interview Larry described Jim and Alice Hammond as: "The most beautiful, most wonderful people on God's Earth". Referring to them as 'mum' and 'dad' he said: "I loved them very much. They loved me and they took me in as their son, even though they never adopted me legally. How could anybody anywhere ask for more?" He added fondly: "I've been very lucky really. I can say I had two mothers." His only real sadness about his unusual parentage was that neither of his mothers lived to see him become famous. In fact it could be argued that he had three mothers as foster sister Fan ended up being largely responsible for his upbringing.

Larry said that, despite his childhood years going down in history as a time of national depression and hardship, he looked back on the 1930s as golden days. He always felt safe, secure and loved, and never once went cold or hungry, even though there was very little money around. It didn't seem to matter because life was simpler and luxuries weren't readily available like they are today, so there was never any thought of 'keeping up with the Joneses'. The Hammonds' home he recalled as "a warm safe place, full of love and caring". What more could a young boy ask for?

It seemed, from a rocky start in his home life, Billy White had landed on his feet, and things were looking good. Tragedy unfortunately was just around the corner. When little Billy was aged just six Alice Hammond, his adoring foster mother, tragically died of cancer after a short illness. In a cruel irony she died on Mothering Sunday, 1930. She was just forty-three. Forty-nine-year-old Jim was literally left holding the baby.

After the horribly sad funeral Ethel White, Billy's real mother, came to the house for a crisis meeting about her son's future. Twenty-two year old May had recently left home to get married and Ethel knew full well that Jim Hammond would have to keep working long hours down the coal mine to keep a roof over their heads, so she said the only answer was to send six-year-old Billy away to boarding school to get a decent education; somewhere he'd be looked after, institutionally at least. May, who liked to take charge of things, had a different solution which, whilst practical, revealed a somewhat unsentimental detachment on her part. She proposed that they should foster Billy out to a different family. Fan said her father's eyes narrowed with anger at both these proposals, and a deep frown furrowed his forehead. "We'll do no such thing!" he declared, trying to remain calm, "He's our Billy. Fan will have to give up her job to look after him." And that was it – the die was cast. The man of the house had spoken. In those days if there was a child around the woman stayed at home to look after it. Fan accepted her lot without argument. She was to be the new matriarch of the house to replace her mother. In any case she loved little Billy as though he was her own. As she said years later: "I just accepted it as what I had to do, because I loved little Billy, and to have had him taken away would have been terrible. He was like a son to me. It was as simple as that."

Barely out of her teens herself Fan was young to be a surrogate mother to a six-year-old, but, in those days, before the welfare state, and before social workers, the caring Hammonds really had no choice. Fan proved to be very maternal – willingly and selflessly sacrificing her own life for Billy's sake. The hardest part for Fan was that she had been 'going steady' for four or five years, and was planning to marry her boyfriend, Bert Phillips. Playing mum to Billy didn't help the path of true love run smooth unfortunately. After her mother's death Fan had to stay in at night to put Billy to bed, and she would only go on dates to the cinema providing little Billy was allowed to tag along. He was always there, tugging at her skirts. In the end Bert got fed up with the constant presence of a needy six-year-old, and gave Fan an ultimatum. She had to choose – Billy or him. With great sadness Fan had to let Bert go off to find a new girlfriend with less baggage. Obviously she often wondered what might have been, but she always said she had no regrets as she adored Billy so much, and she also knew her 'father' needed looking after, so her place was at home with them. Fan never did marry, devoting her entire life to Billy, unlike her older sister May, who had already managed to make a life for herself and soon had a family of her own.

For the first couple of years of their married life May and her new husband, Charlie Roberts, lived in the house next door, so she was able to pop in every day to see Fan and to help look after Billy and their 'dad'. It wasn't too long before they moved a little further away, ending up in Coventry, but May provided invaluable support for Fan in those first difficult months. After that Fan was on her own to run the home and bring up Billy.

Fan was a saint really. Remember Jim Hammond wasn't her real dad, he was her step-father; and Billy wasn't even her real brother, just a child her parents had fostered; and yet she willingly sacrificed everything to look after both of them. Larry never forgot that.

Money was always tight in the Hammond household, with only Jim's wages coming in, and because there was no benefits system in those days for additional help. However coal miner Jim continued to work hard doing long hours down the pit, allowing Fan to be at home keeping-house and cooking a hot meal when Billy returned home hungry from school. Thanks to Fan, and her father Jim, Billy never wanted for anything, and he always remembered his childhood as a very happy time. Larry never forgot Fan's devotion or the sacrifices she had made on his behalf. He continued to shower her with gifts and attention right up to his death. In the famous and successful years on tour Larry would always pop into a shop in each new town to buy something nice for 'the little lady', which he would give to Fan upon his return home. They lived under the same roof together virtually all of Larry's life.

Fan prided herself in keeping little Billy immaculate – freshly-polished well-heeled boots, laundered white shirts, and so on, where many of his school chums were much more urchin-like in appearance. Billy was high maintenance though. Fan said he was very fussy about his clothes, throwing a tantrum and demanding more than one clean shirt a day if he got so much as a small mark on the one he was wearing. He was always fastidious. Fan remembered how he liked everything to be tidy at home, and she said he used to follow her round with his own dustpan and brush, helping her with the housework. She said when he went off to school he was always very smart. His shoes would have a shine you could see your face in, and his clothes were spotless. Other scruffier boys would sometimes point at him and tease him, but he'd just stick his nose in the air and say to himself: "Never mind – I'm going to be a famous star one day...". He somehow knew that was his destiny.

Billy was also a sickly child, and had to be regularly nursed through toothaches, earaches and every common childhood ailment going, plus a few less common ones, like Scarlet Fever and rheumatics in his feet. Larry fondly remembered that Fan would always buy him sweets when he was poorly, and he often spoke about her being so caring that she'd sometimes wrap his skinny little legs up in cotton wool to keep them warm when he was ill in bed during the cold winter months. Fan said he was hardly ever at school because he caught every disease going: "I can remember thinking sometimes – he's not going to survive. God's been good to you Fan, but he's going to take your little lad away from you this time. But mercifully it never happened." Fan said he was worth all the hard work and heartache however, because he was such a loving child.

Because Jim Hammond was working long hours down the pit, and Fan was so attentive to Billy's every need, plus all the regular visits from May and his real mum, 'Aunty Ethel', it meant that little Billy was brought up in a female-dominated environment. He was a great listener and he was fascinated by the way his 'sisters', his real mother, and their friends and neighbours all gossiped and tittle-tattled. It doesn't take a great deal of imagination to see that this was already sowing the early seeds of the much-loved Larry Grayson act.

From the word go little Billy White proved he was a born performer. Nobody knew where it came from. Fan said he was stage-struck from the start. When he was still only about two years old she and her mother would take him to the local toyshop every Friday. He'd learned that if he did a little dance they would buy him something. "He was quite a performer even in those days" she said. In a 1973 television interview Larry himself recalled jumping on the table as young as three years old to sing "The Holy City", a religious Victorian ballad, for anybody who would listen. He claimed, in typical Larry style, his enthusiastic singing was the reason the neighbours moved away. Alice and Jim loved it though and encouraged him, getting him to sing along to their old wind-up gramophone records. If it was a fast number Billy would invent a little dance to do on top of the heavy kitchen table.

The Hammonds had quite an impressive collection of shellac or wax 78rpm records and Larry fondly remembered the huge wind-up gramophone with the big green horn "taking up nearly half the kitchen". Jim would patiently sit puffing on his pipe while Billy played record after record, occasionally telling him to turn the horn round the other way if it was a particularly raucous recording. The other source of home entertainment back then was the 'wireless' (radio). Billy particularly loved the stories during *Children's Hour* with Uncle Mac. They would all sit round the wireless set and close their eyes to create the pictures for themselves.

2

... school is suffered... but showbiz beckons...

During his reception year at Abbey Green Infants School, still just five years old, Billy 'Hammond' White took to a proper stage for the very first time. Every Christmas each class put on a playlet, the older ones always performing a scene from *A Christmas Carol* by Charles Dickens. The little ones were responsible for the annual nativity play, which the whole school had to attend. Their strict teacher Miss Farmer was in charge of the casting, and Larry always said that this was the only audition he ever attended in the whole of his career. With his hair slicked down with water, and trying to look taller than everybody else, Billy waited with bated breath to see if there was a part for him. Joseph, Mary, Archangel Gabriel, the innkeeper were all announced, even the kids playing shepherds, camels, sheep and donkeys. Finally she said: "And you Hammond will be a wise man". His little heart pounded with excitement. He had been discovered!

Billy's first concern was what he should wear for this pivotal role. The teacher said the wise men should wear cloaks, so he raced home to elicit Fan's help. She took down a heavy blue velvet draught curtain from the front door, removed the brass rings, and washed it. Billy wasn't satisfied though and hounded Fan to make improvements to his cloak. Dutifully she found cotton wool with which to make an 'ermine' collar, but Billy still wasn't happy, so she bought crepe paper, tinsel, tin foil, cardboard and glue and cleverly decorated the cloak, then made a jewelled crown and even a 'chain' to go around his neck. At last Billy felt this was a costume fit for a King. The first time the rather austere Miss Farmer saw him in his flamboyant outfit, during the dress rehearsal, she looked over her spectacles at him disapprovingly and said: "Right Hammond – you can take some of that lot off – you are supposed to be a wise man, not a Christmas tree..."

Somewhat deflated Billy was still determined to steal the show. The wise men were instructed by Miss Farmer to enter with their gifts for the baby Jesus, then place their offerings by the manger, smile at Mary and move out of the way to the back of the stage, along with the shepherds, behind the sheep, camels and donkeys. On the day of the actual performance Billy was terribly excited by the presence of the audience, so he managed to manoeuvre himself to the front of the other two wise men to make more of an impact with his entrance. Having got the audience's admiring glances he didn't much fancy having to blend in to the background however, so he decided to stay exactly where he was. Miss Farmer reprimanded him sternly afterwards: "Just what did you think you were doing stuck out in front of everybody like that Hammond? This was supposed to be a nativity play about Mary, Joseph and the birth of the baby Jesus. With you stuck in the way nobody could see them or the manger! Do as you are told next time. It's supposed to be a serious play and there you were stuck out in front of everybody grinning like a Cheshire Cat! Now off you go... Oh and have a merry Christmas..." Never mind the birth of baby Jesus, Miss Farmer had just witnessed the birth of a star.

Just a matter of days after his own scene-stealing stage debut the Hammonds took Billy to the professional theatre for the first time to see *Babes in the Wood* at The Nuneaton Hippodrome. He was so excited by the prospect that he didn't get a wink of sleep the night before. Some five-year-olds would have found the experience of their first pantomime overwhelming, but not little Billy White. He found the magnificent splendour of the theatre, the buzz of the audience and the live orchestra captivating, but when the house lights dimmed and the plush red velvet curtains parted to reveal a brightly lit colourful world of singing, dancing, comedy, tragedy and magic he was completely mesmerised. He didn't understand about makeup and wigs, so he thought all these people with painted faces and brightly coloured shocks of hair really looked like that all the time. Larry remembered thinking this was "the magic land", and that he didn't want to so much as blink in case he missed anything. From that day he just knew that was where he was born to be. If he hadn't been hooked on showbusiness before, he certainly was now. He said for months afterwards all he could think about was that show, and how he couldn't wait for the next Christmas and his next pantomime.

Larry said many times in later life that all he ever wanted to be was a star, right from his earliest childhood memories. Having seen how it was done professionally he now wanted to put on more polished and properly produced shows at home. So his biggest thrill, when he was still a very young boy, was sweet-talking Fan into scrubbing out the brick-built washhouse at the back of the house, and moving the heavy old iron mangle (clothes wringer to anybody under sixty) to one side, covering it with a white sheet. She then had to set up improvised curtains for him. "Not just anything, mind" she once said, "They had to be good curtains". Billy would put up a poster advertising tonight's performance, opening the box office for advance ticket sales. He'd charge neighbouring kids the princely sum of a returnable pop bottle (you got money back on empty bottles in those days), or a couple of cigarette cards, to see him stage impromptu shows, concerts and playlets. His party-pieces included the Johnny Mercer and Hoagy Carmichael song "Lazy Bones", made famous by The Mills Brothers, and a tap dance on an upturned steel dolly tub. He'd even send Fan out to the baker's to scrounge a stale cake which she could warm in the oven to give to his audience in the interval.

Billy liked to have everything just right and make his amateur home productions as close to a proper visit to the professional theatre as he possibly could. In the 1930s there was a fashion for theatres and cinemas to gently spray perfume over the audience during the interval. Presumably warm audiences were quite smelly in the days when a bath was a weekly event. Fan vividly remembered coming in to the room where Billy was putting on a show for his school chums one day and seeing a boy looking half asleep on the front row, then, to her horror, she smelt gas. Billy had turned on the gas tap to emulate the hissing of the perfume sprays down at The Hippodrome. Fan said Billy nearly gassing his audience was the talk of the street for weeks.

Years later Larry told a journalist: "As a kid I was mad about concerts. I used to organise my own shows and, of course, I had to be the star. I would recruit my audience from school chums at Abbey Green Juniors. If they wouldn't come I punched them!"

It seems he really wasn't averse to resorting to physical violence in the pursuit of artistic excellence. In a happy reunion with four of his old classmates for an ITV celebration of Larry's 60th birthday Elsie Lee laughingly remembered being 'bashed' by Billy (as he still was back then) for refusing to play an ugly sister in his version of Cinderella one Christmas, and Joan Bowles remembered he was always smacking her for not doing exactly as she was told when he was staging his concerts.

He would also put on shows for the family in the front room, "Like 'An Evening With'..." Larry once told an amused Michael Parkinson during an interview on Parkie's famous BBC chat show. By the age of six his repertoire contained several well-known love songs of the day. His proud foster father Jim decided the boy must be nothing short of a genius.

Performing, dressing up, and 'showing off' was anathema to his surrogate sisters and foster parents however, so it was clearly in his genes somewhere, and didn't in any way come from the Hammond household. Even his real mother Ethel, who was quite musical and enjoyed a bit of glamour, found Billy's burning desire to go on stage bewildering. A life in the theatre was still considered somewhat disreputable in those days. People who knew Ethel's complicated parental situation would say: "Poor Ethel. As if she hasn't had enough trouble, and now that son of hers, the one 'sent down from the angels', wants to go on the stage. It must be a judgment on her... Perhaps he'll grow out of it..."

In fact the whole family's attitude, according to Larry, was exactly that: "Ignore him. He'll grow out of it. It's just a phase he's going through!" Fan was rather prone to amusing malapropisms and she used to say it was a 'phrase' he was going through. However Billy's blossoming love of showbusiness was far from a passing phase or phrase, it was his raison d'etre. His passion for all things showbiz was further fuelled by frequent visits with Fan to 'the pictures', as the cinema was called in those days.

Billy wasn't interested in the 'Tuppenny Rush' however. That was the local name for the mixed bag of cheap comedy shorts, cartoons and tacky serials which were on offer for hordes of over-excited noisy kids on a Saturday morning for a couple of old pennies. He said he was far too stuck-up to watch rubbish like *Flash Gordon*. What he loved were the proper feature-length films made for an adult audience, with big Hollywood stars like Clark Gable, Joan Crawford, Bette Davis and Eddie Cantor. The trouble was the tickets for those films were expensive. He used to get some pocket money, but he'd also run errands for people and return empty pop and beer bottles to the grocer's shop for extra cash in order to finance his regular cinema visits.

In the 1930s there were six thriving Nuneaton picture houses, all just about within walking distance of Stanley Crescent, so there was plenty of choice for a movie obsessed little boy. Those were the days of a supporting 'B' movie and a newsreel to turn the main feature into a full programme of entertainment. Billy would go two or three times a week, often staying in his seat at the end of the first house to watch the whole screening twice over. He would sit wide-eyed at the flickering images on the silver screen, losing himself in this magical glamorous make-believe world of heroes and villains, slapstick comedians and matinee idols, singers and hoofers, cowboys and Indians, lovers and fighters. As soon as he was old enough to read he never missed a copy of his favourite cinema magazines *Picturegoer* and *Picture Show*'.

Such was his passion for the cinema that his knowledge of films and film-making became encyclopaedic. He absorbed everything. Not just the names of the stars and supporting actors, but also the names of the directors and the composers of the soundtracks. He got to the point where he could even tell you, from the grain of the celluloid film, the musical arrangements, and the cinematography as the first frames came up, whether the movie had been made in Hollywood by the likes of 20th Century Fox, or in Britain by say Gainsborough Pictures. His love of films from that innocent romantic Hollywood-dominated era never waned. In fact his stage name Grayson paid tribute to one of his many Hollywood heroines, singer and actress Kathryn Grayson. In middle-age Larry stopped going to the cinema all together, much preferring to watch his old black and white favourites on Sunday afternoons at home in front of the television with Fan. He was quite a prude at heart, and he couldn't stand the sex, violence, nudity and bad language that had crept into modern movie making. He mourned the passing of a golden age.

Because Billy genuinely was a sickly child, and prone to illness, if he said he was too poorly for school Fan couldn't always tell if it was genuine or whether he was 'swinging the lead' to get a day off. He used this to his advantage sometimes to squeeze in another trip to the cinema. He'd come downstairs clutching his stomach and say: "Ooh Fan I'm too poorly to go to school today", then three hours later he'd be saying: "Lovely film on at The Palace today Fan..." She said it was hard to be cross with him though because she knew how much pleasure he got out of his visits to the cinema: "He knew those film stars like he knew his alphabet..."

During the school holidays he'd deliberately mooch around looking miserable and getting under Fan's feet. She knew exactly what his game was, but he'd always win. Eventually she'd give him a few coins. His face would brighten immediately and off he'd dash to the cinema. She used to tell him that it wasn't healthy to spend all day in a dark picture house – he should be out in the sunshine and the fresh air – but her advice fell on deaf ears. He couldn't think of a single outdoor activity that could possibly match up to the thrill of immersing himself in the glamour of Hollywood...

He even loved looking at the evocative colourful film posters outside the cinemas, heralding the latest releases with all his favourite stars. One thing that really annoyed little Billy though was the X certificate on adult films, because seeing that wretched 'X' on a cinema poster meant he couldn't go and see the latest picture house offering, as that was the equivalent of an '18' certificate nowadays. One of his favourite Hollywood actors was Boris Karloff, who was of course most famous for his scary horror films. If a Boris Karloff film came on down at The Scala or The Palace and it had an X certificate this would make little Billy stamp his feet and throw a real tantrum. Fan said that Billy was basically a good and loving little lad, but he was prone to having occasional quite scary tantrums if he didn't get all his own way. She blamed her big soft teddy bear of a stepfather, who did have a tendency to spoil his foster son and indulge his every whim.

The simple truth was Jim Hammond absolutely doted on his foster son, young Billy, particularly after Alice died. The feeling was mutual. Larry once said after Jim's death: "I adored my 'dad'. He had the bluest eyes of anyone I've ever met and, in the truest sense of the word, he was a gentleman. I never ever heard him raise his voice to anyone – he was always calm and kind." Larry had fond memories of spending quality time with Jim during the school holidays. If Jim was doing the afternoon shift down the pit they would have a walk along the canal bank after breakfast, but Billy preferred him to be on nights, because then they'd have the afternoons to explore Spring Wood and Weddington Meadows where they'd pick bunches of violets and honeysuckle to take home for Fan.

Any spare coppers Jim managed to save from his meagre pay packet were put in a jar, then, when there was enough, the coins were given to Fan to take little Billy to the seaside for the weekend. Over the years they went off all over the place – Portsmouth, Southsea, and Blackpool, which was always Billy's favourite of course, because of all the theatres there.

All the time little Billy White attended Abbey Green Infants & Junior School he appeared on the class register as Billy Hammond, to avoid any awkward questions being asked about his parentage. Larry always described himself as a very thin, deathly pale, sickly child who didn't much like school – probably the only thing he had in common with most of his friends. He said he always liked to look immaculate, all neat, clean and tidy, unlike most of his rough and tumble football-playing male classmates with their mucky faces, muddy boots and grazed knees. The highlight of his academic year was donning his pristine white pumps for the annual school ritual of skipping round the Maypole every spring. Having heard all this you could be forgiven for thinking that Billy must have been bullied, as he was effeminate and inherently camp from a very early age. But you'd be wrong. Funnily enough he was no push-over. In fact he had a short fuse and could deliver a well-aimed right hook when it was required, so he could defend himself against bullies. He was also very popular, so school days were generally happy, if not terribly productive academically.

As we all know kids can be very cruel to one another sometimes. Larry said some of his classmates would occasionally tease him about not having a real mum, and Fan not being his real sister. He said they'd unkindly taunt him about having been 'found'. Of course that led to fall-outs and the odd fight, but Fan said he always made it up with his chums the very next minute. In hindsight he was philosophical about their jibes and said they didn't mean any harm: "You know how kids are...", but he admitted they hurt at the time. He said he was very sensitive as a schoolboy, and the cruel jibes about his parentage brought on a childhood stammer, but he used to reassure himself with the certain knowledge that: "I will be a star one day, and then none of this will matter..."

Billy was a bit of an oddity in his class for all sorts of reasons, but he had one kindred spirit in a like-minded boy named Tom Proctor. They had started school on the same day and were put into the same class, striking up a special bond almost immediately. People often mistook them for brothers as they had the same slim build and fair hair. Tom and Billy became inseparable best friends and soulmates from being just five years old, and remained extremely close until Tom's tragic and untimely death, aged just twenty-one. Tom Proctor had the same obsession with the cinema and the glamour of Hollywood, and they both had the same loathing of sport, woodwork, and anything that involved getting their hands dirty at school.

The two boys were academic equals as well, but unfortunately that wasn't saying very much. Their school divided classes up into streams according to academic ability. A, B, C and R streams. Tom and Billy never made it out of the 'R' stream, which was the lowest of the low. The brighter kids used to tease them that the 'R' stood for 'rejects', but it almost certainly stood for 'remedial'. The trouble was they were far more interested in discussing the plot of the latest Bette Davis film than trying to figure out the seemingly unfathomable and, to them, pointless mysteries of simple arithmetic. Billy would do impressions of his favourite film stars in class, much to the amusement of Tom, and much to the irritation of their teachers.

The two rascals also shared the same sense of humour, giggling helplessly at anything and everything. In the playground they would be in a hysterical world all of their own, crying with laughter at things the others simply couldn't comprehend. Classmates would say: "You two are a pair of idiots – you're always cackling about something!" Billy, with a witty put-down that would have made Oscar Wilde envious, would retort: "Shut your cake'ole!". Naturally enough their shared sense of the ridiculous, leading to fits of the giggles, got them into trouble at school on a regular basis. In those days every minor misdemeanour resulted in a stinging stroke or two of the cane across the outstretched palms of their hands. A giggling Billy and Tom were for ever being told to come out to the front of the class... "And bring the cane with you...".

The two best friends were constantly in trouble for talking, giggling, skiving out of doing anything at all in woodwork classes, slacking at sport, not to mention the irresistible temptation to cheat on tests and homework, in order to cover up for their lack of interest in anything remotely academic. All the above meant standing side by side, holding out their hands time and time again for the cane. Even that made them giggle.

Being an austere period in British history the Abbey Green boys were taught self-sufficiency in the form of gardening classes, while the girls did cookery. The idea was to teach the lads how to grow their own vegetables. Billy and Tom didn't much like getting their hands dirty, and wished they could join the girls learning how to make pies and cakes. Pairs of boys were each given a small plot to cultivate together. For obvious reasons Billy and Tom were split up, but Billy got lucky and was paired up with a boy called Roland Neal, who was an expert gardener, having learned every trick in the book from his green-fingered father on his two large allotments. Billy told his new gardening partner that he would frankly be more of a hindrance, so somehow he persuaded Roland to do all the work while he dreamed of Hollywood and pretended to look busy. One day though Billy was caught doing nothing by Mr Westbrook, the teacher in charge of the school garden, who said: "Make yourself useful Hammond – do some weeding! And do it properly boy!". Billy had no choice but to get his hands dirty on this occasion. A short while later there was a strangulated scream from Roland Neal, which brought Mr Westbrook running back. Billy, who didn't know a dandelion from a dahlia, had efficiently pulled up all the weeds, but he'd also pulled up every single one of Roland's healthy young vegetable plants. From that day on Billy was banned from the school garden and was made to sit in class reading a book. Quietly Billy was delighted, and his friend Tom was extremely envious.

Larry's prowess as a gardener never really improved, and neither did his plant recognition skills. When he became rich and famous he had a gardener. One day Larry went out to chat to him and spotted lots of dainty pretty leaves, so he asked when they come into bloom. "They don't!" said his gardener, "They're carrots!".

The only thing that peas-in-a-pod Billy White and Tom Proctor didn't have in common, it seems, was their ability to get out of bed in the morning. Fan would get Billy up bright and early, and he would punctually call for his friend on his way to school, but Tom was invariably still in bed, dead to the world, so Billy would have to continue his journey alone. When the class attendance register was called Billy would have to tell the teacher that Tom was still in bed, much to her displeasure. Billy would then get the giggles as he looked out of the window and spotted his dishevelled friend running full pelt in through the gates and across the playground, still half dressed. Tom would get another stroke or two of the cane from their formidable teacher for being late, and poor Billy would get exactly the same punishment for finding the whole thing so amusing. Even when Tom did eventually get behind his desk he was still half asleep and would doze his way through most of the morning.

Tom never did grow out of his inability to get up in the morning. It got him into constant hot water at school, and it got him into even more trouble when he started work. One can only imagine the fury of fearsome army Sergeant Majors when he was called up for National Service during World War II. His tardiness even ended up being the death of him – quite literally.

Larry told a journalist that he never really liked school because he was always in trouble for talking too much. "I'd be sitting in class making arrangements for my new concert. I'd be whispering across the classroom, and the teacher would pull me up – they were very strict you know – then they'd send me out. At least they taught me how to walk on and off!" Forty years later he admitted he was still afflicted with the same problem of talking too much: "Somehow though I've talked my way to The London Palladium".

In the same interview Larry recalled: "One of my most powerful memories of Abbey Green Juniors was the time I got blackmailed. Yes, blackmailed! The teachers had put a notice up in the playground about spitting, and I accidentally dropped a gobstopper from my mouth. One boy spotted me and threatened to tell the teachers that I'd spat, if I didn't give him my sweets. He kept it up for weeks!"

The only bit of proper schooling that Billy White actually enjoyed happened every Friday afternoon, when Miss Booth would read chapters from Charles Dickens novels to the whole class for half an hour. He was enthralled. His disdain for day school was tempered however by a love of Sunday School, which he enthusiastically attended at St Mary's Abbey Church. Again he was enthralled by the stories from *The Bible*, and he enjoyed learning and singing all the hymns. Not too surprisingly Tom Proctor was never out of bed in time to attend Sunday School, but another pal of Billy's attended the Sunday School at the local Baptist Chapel in Manor Road. This sounded even more attractive to Billy, so he suddenly switched from church to chapel. The transfer was very satisfactory as the Baptist chapel gave their Sunday School kids occasional treats of jelly, ice cream, cake and orangeade, and they got gold stars and prizes for attendance. Perhaps if his day school had done the same he might have dragged himself out of the 'R' stream. The other good thing about Sunday school was there was no dratted cane...

Besides the much anticipated annual pantomime, the highlights of the year for young Billy and his friend Tom were the visiting fairs and circuses. All of these things were an exhilarating assault on the senses. The brash bright colours, the evocative music, the unique smells, and even the tastes of the treats on offer. Young Billy was mesmerised by the circus animals, the fairground 'freaks', the white knuckle rides, the pumping sounds of the steam organs. In 1935, when Billy was twelve, the Hammonds moved to a slightly larger house in Harefield Road, which even had its own garden. Better yet though it overlooked the site where a small travelling fair had its winter base. From his bedroom window Billy could watch the magic being created – the rides, game stalls and sideshows being built, repaired and re-painted for the next season. Every Saturday evening the tools and paint brushes would be put away so that Holland's Fair could open for a few hours for the local kids. Billy loved watching the fun and hearing the happy cries mingling with the music, and seeing the bright lights whirling and flickering across the walls and ceiling of his bedroom.

At the age of eleven, along with most of his friends from Abbey Green Juniors, Billy had moved up to Manor Park secondary school. It didn't really make a whole lot of difference to his education however, because he was never going to be academically inclined. There was only one ambition he had in life, and that didn't require any passing of exams. One day in the confines of the playground at Manor Park, a group of small boys were discussing what they would do when they left school. Several said: "A miner, like me dad". Others, with a little more foresight and ambition, plumped for things like: bus driver, train driver, signalman, soldier... but Billy White left them all agape when he announced that when he grew up he was going to be 'a star'. Larry later said that when the inevitable hoots of derision died down he was then subjected to an interrogation. "Can you sing?" ... "Not very well..." ... "Can you dance?" ... "Not really..." ... "Well can you play a musical instrument?" ... "Well, no..." ... "Well you're not going to be a star then are you?!" ... His unflinching response was simple: "I am SO going to be a star!"

And that is precisely what cuts stars apart from the rest of us mere mortals – complete and utter unwavering self-belief. I do hope some of those incredulous mocking Manor Park boys lived to see Billy 'Hammond' White become one of the biggest stars in Britain, without ever really being able to sing, dance or play a musical instrument.

He was quite envious of some his less ambitious and less talented classmates who were able to take tap dancing classes and singing lessons, as well as those who were learning to play musical instruments. Some of his friends even had the luxury of a piano in the front parlour. It was the time of The Great Depression, and a humble coal miner like Jim Hammond simply couldn't afford to pay for these extra-curricular classes, and he certainly couldn't afford to buy a piano, much as he would have liked to have encouraged his talented young foster son. Billy White wasn't deterred however, and carried on dreaming of one day being a star. In any case the two things he had above everybody else were things money can't buy – raw talent and bags of determination.

3

... turning professional... and the outbreak of war...

As Billy White and his best friend Tom Proctor had never made it out of the educationally-challenged 'R' stream they had to leave school at the age of fourteen and find work. Billy made up a story for friends at school that he was going to work behind the bacon counter in the Co-Op store, just to get them off his back about his future plans, but in reality he had no such intention. All he could ever think about was a life on the stage. His doting foster father Jim and Fan were always keen to help him, and were encouraging about his ambitions to be a performer, but they didn't have any experience or knowledge of the professional world of showbusiness. This meant that they were woefully ill-equipped to advise a stage-struck fourteen year old school leaver, when that time inevitably came... but fate was about to offer a helping hand.

Just a few weeks before Billy was due to finish school the Freeman family moved into the house next door to the Hammonds' home in Harefield Road, Nuneaton. The family unit was Alf Freeman, who was an archetypal rotund ruddy-faced jolly butcher; his cheerful wife Nell, who was taller and more slender, with long auburn hair; and their daughter Freda, who was a couple of years older than Billy. Freda was more like her father in build and was described by straight-talking Fan as: 'a big girl'. It was immediately apparent that they were a warm, friendly, gregarious and kind-hearted family and were going to make good neighbours. Billy couldn't have imagined how good. In no time at all the Hammonds and the Freemans were getting on famously and Nell Freeman heard that Billy ran errands for a few coppers, so she asked him to get her husband a pot of white paint. When he returned with the paint he was invited into the house and he immediately spotted an upright piano with sheet music open on its stand. He excitedly asked Mrs Freeman if she was a pianist. "No dear, our Freda plays. She does an act with her dad." Billy couldn't believe his ears – fellow performers next door! He could hardly get the words out fast enough, asking if they were in the theatre and what they did. Nell told the excited fourteen-year-old that her husband and daughter had a musical act which they performed in the local clubs at weekends. This was thrilling news, especially when Nell asked him if he would like to come round some time to watch them practise. True to her word, a few days later, Mrs Freeman came knocking and asked if Billy would like to come round to listen to Freda and Alf who were about to rehearse something new for their act.

Freda played the accompaniment while Alf sang in his rich tenor voice, in the style of Richard Tauber. Freda then sang soprano, in the style of film star Deanna Durbin. Billy was entranced, telling them how much he wanted to be on the stage himself one day. Nell Freeman was already taking to young Billy, welcoming him into their family, so she encouraged her daughter to teach him a song or two. Freda had a day job at Courtaulds in Coventry, but Billy would eagerly wait for her return in the evening, hoping she would call round to give him another singing lesson, which she often did. He was a quick learner and he only had to hear a song once to start picking it up. He always had a good ear for picking up tunes, and even accents, as well as amusing turns of phrase. After one of these lessons Alf Freeman, who had been eyeing Billy's progress, suddenly said: "He ought to come along with us one night and do a little act of his own." Billy couldn't believe his ears. He was so thrilled he ran home to tell Fan, then dashed off to tell his best friend Tom Proctor, who had by then got himself a mundane job at Sketchley's Dye Works in Hinckley. Tom was as excited by the news as Billy was.

Years later Larry said those precious few weeks after leaving school changed his life. He owed everything to the Freemans. It's no wonder Larry ended up believing in guardian angels. Fan and the Hammonds had always been there watching over him, and looking after him, now the Freemans were taking him under their wing, spotting and nurturing his blossoming talent while he was still only in his early teens. They were so kindly and welcoming he soon began calling Mr & Mrs Freeman 'Aunty

Nell' and 'Uncle Alf', even though they were no more than next door neighbours in reality.

Alf, who had a keen sense of humour himself, had spotted Billy's natural flare for comedy, so he got Freda to teach the promising young lad next door a selection of funny songs made famous by a music hall comedian and pantomime dame called Clarkson Rose. Comedy was something their act had lacked up until now, so this new departure was going to be a welcome addition. Billy rehearsed his new comedy song repertoire intensively with Freda for a week or so, until Alf thrillingly announced that he thought their new protégé was ready for his first taste of professional showbusiness.

As a try-out Aunty Nell said he should join Alf and Freda at an old folks' home where they were making an unpaid appearance. When she told Billy that his first performance was to be the very next day he was paralysed with fear and just stood there repeating: "I can't! I can't!". Nell came right up to him and gave him a bit of tough love. She slapped him, saying: "Pull yourself together! You are going!" They then sat Billy down and gave him a glass of port to calm his nerves, reassuring him that he could do it, that he knew the song, and that he had to just get up there and do what he was born to do. Larry later said how grateful he was to Nell for that slap and her firm encouragement, because it put an end to stage fright getting the better of him, or stopping him performing. He said if he'd pulled out of that first performance with Alf and Freda none of the rest of it would have ever happened, and Larry Grayson would have never existed. Nell's tough love didn't stop the nerves, but it helped him overcome them. The next day, as he donned his little hat to sing his first song at the old folks' home, Aunty Nell gave him some sound advice: "Remember – be cheeky. Have personality and a twinkle in your eye." I think it's fair to say that Nell Freeman's advice served him well for the rest of his career.

Fourteen-year-old Billy's first professional engagement came shortly after that steep learning curve at the old folks' home. It was actually at a wedding reception at The Fife Street Working Men's Club, quite close to where they all lived in Nuneaton. That life-changing night he performed just two comic songs: "So I Got On My Bike and I Cycled Away" and "Walking Through Mockingbird Lane". Larry still remembered, years later, having his heart in his mouth with nerves, standing in the wings waiting to make his entrance for his first performance as a 'pro'. However, just like any born entertainer, it didn't take long before the thrill of the waves of audience laughter and applause overshadowed any stage fright, and he was hooked. As he himself once said about that professional debut: "I felt wonderful when I got my first applause, and I thought to myself there and then, 'This the life! This is what I am here for!'...".

Fan remembered seeing tears in her stepfather's eyes as Jim Hammond watched their Billy walking out on to the stage, cutting quite a dash in a dazzling white blazer and flannels, singing and making people laugh. She couldn't hide her own immense pride either when friends and neighbours kept leaning over and asking "Is that your boy Fan, is that really your boy?"

Billy's very welcome share of the Freemans' fee was five shillings (twenty-five pence). At a time when delivery boys were earning around twelve shillings for a full week, this was a princely sum for ten minutes' work. Fan, canny and careful as ever, said "Right Billy – that's half a crown for you to spend... and half a crown goes into your Post Office savings account..." Half a crown was two shillings and sixpence, as those over the age of sixty will remember. To anybody under sixty it was a coin equivalent to twelve-and-a-half pence in current decimalised currency. He learned from that simple lesson and, all through his life, even in the successful days, he always put half his fee into his savings account, which left him very comfortably off in his later years, long after the work dried up. He was always a shrewd investor and never took gambles with money. Of course he always looked after Fan financially, even before the big money started rolling in.

The word quickly spread around the local working men's clubs about the funny young lad who sang the cheeky songs, so new bookings with Alf Freeman and Freda started to fill up his diary. Billy put in the work with Freda and learned more saucy little rhymes and songs, most of which he probably didn't fully understand himself, but he knew they made the miners and their wives cackle and clap. All the more so because they were coming from the lips of this strangely angelic looking young lad, and particularly when his saucy performances evolved to include various camp and mildly suggestive gestures and hand actions. His signature song soon became "In the Bushes at the Bottom of the Garden", which alluded to the goings-on in those said bushes by spooning couples, Peeping Tom, Adam & Eve, and even next door's tom cat. Harmless stuff by today's 'anything goes' standards, but it was pretty daring for its time, in that same cheeky vein as the positively outrageous things George Formby saw when he was cleaning windows.

Billy was a quick learner. Not only were all these club bookings giving him invaluable experience of playing to all sorts of different audiences, but he was also seeing other acts work, and learning what went down well and what didn't, allowing him to hone and develop his own unique style. In those formative years he learned his impeccable comedy timing – the value of the knowing pause, the look, the raised eyebrow and the camp gesture – allowing the audience to do the work and doubling the laugh.

Now that he was a professional performer Billy decided he needed a stage name. He thought Billy Hammond didn't sound like a comedy entertainer, so he looked through a copy of *The Stage* newspaper for inspiration. There he spotted the actress wife of humorist Cyril Fletcher, who worked as Betty Astell. He liked the sound of her name and for several weeks he was billed as Billy Astell. (In a quirk of showbusiness fate he would become a close friend of Cyril and Betty, many years later, when they became neighbours in Torquay.) Just a few weeks later however, in another copy of *The Stage*, he saw a write-up and review of the pantomime *Robinson Crusoe* at The Grand Theatre in Blackpool, which featured Helen Breen as the Principal Boy. He liked the sound of her name even better. For nearly twenty years his stage name was Billy Breen. He thought it sounded 'clean', what ever that means. People have wrongly thought that he borrowed the name from a popular singer of the time called Bobby Breen, but it actually came from a little known English singer and actress called Helen Breen.

With real money in his pocket for the first time in his life Billy was no longer reliant on hand-outs from Jim and Fan, and was able to indulge his passions for the cinema and theatre even more. Off he'd go on the bus to the magnificent Hippodrome Theatre in Coventry to see all the big name radio comedians and variety stars of the time. They were all inspirational to him as an evolving performer himself – the likes of Sandy Powell, Jewel & Warris, Wee Georgie Wood, Wilson Keppel & Betty, Old Mother Riley, Elsie & Doris Waters, and the sublime Robb Wilton. He also loved all the musicals, which were often try-outs for London's West End theatres. Tickets were one shilling (five pence).

The only 'proper job' Billy ever seemed to have after he left school was in a shoe shop, but that didn't last very long: two days, Larry once told a television interviewer, claiming he was 'let go' for selling somebody two left Wellington boots. The anecdote has the whiff of typical Grayson-esque embellishment, but either way his shoe sales career was short-lived. In truth he just walked out after his first unhappy days selling shoes and refused to go back. Many widower dads of that period would have given him a clip round the ear and told him to knuckle under to this 'proper job', but big-hearted Jim Hammond always had a soft spot for his foster son and indulged him yet again. Even Fan thought Billy should be made to go back to the shoe shop and give it another go, but Jim just said: "Leave him. If he doesn't like it we can't force the lad to do it." Billy's inability to hold down a normal job didn't really matter though because he was born to entertain.

With his lack of interest in any other sort of job, and his blossoming career on stage with Alf Freeman and his daughter Freda, Billy White had left school, still aged just fourteen, changed his name to Billy Breen, and had become a professional entertainer. He was living the dream.

Life was sweet for a couple of years, but then in 1939 storm clouds started to gather over Europe, and life for everyone in Britain began to change dramatically and irreversibly. Nuneaton council workmen erected an Anderson Shelter in the garden of the Hammonds' household, and sandbags and gasmasks were issued to protect the family from what ever Hitler had to throw at them, should war break out, which was looking increasingly likely. Rationing was enforced and, as summer passed and the days got shorter, blackout curtains were put over the windows and doors.

When the inevitable Second World War was finally declared in September 1939, the worst thing for sixteen-year-old Billy, much to his horror, was that the theatres, cinemas, and all other places of entertainment were to be immediately closed, boarded up and blacked out "for the duration". Fortunately it was quickly realised that this dispiriting and drastic measure was bad for British morale, so the Government back-tracked and all the theatres and cinemas re-opened again just twelve days after the announcement of this total black-out – much to Billy's relief. Entertainment turned out to be the one thing that kept the British upper lip stiff, and lifted the nation's spirits with some much-needed light relief from the horrors, depravation and miseries of war. The only small concession to the hostilities was that the cinemas and theatres opened their doors half an hour earlier, so that people could be safely home before 10pm when there was the greatest risk of air raids.

Fortunately the Government's U-turn on theatre closures also meant that Billy Breen could carry on performing in the pubs and clubs with Alf Freeman and Freda. The act was going from strength to strength and improving all the time. It was shrewd 'Aunty Nell' Freeman who came up with the idea which took things even further. She pointed out that as a trio they were just one of three acts who appeared on the bill every night in the clubs. Nell figured that if they could bring in another couple of performers they could market themselves as a full-blown concert party and offer a whole night of self-contained entertainment, with no need for other rival support acts. This of course meant they could command three times the fee. Alf thought this was a splendid idea and said they should look for a more contemporary singer of more popular style songs, or maybe a dancer, plus a versatile showman pianist.

Billy, now moving more in showbusiness circles, told Alf he had two friends who possibly fitted the bill. Firstly there was Ronnie Hollis who worked in the local branch of 'Weaver to Wearer', a cut-price menswear chain. Ronnie had been in a choir, so he could sing a bit, but, more importantly, he was an accomplished pianist, playing everything from the classics to popular music; and he could tap dance. In fact he could dance while he played the piano, which is not an easy feat! Alf auditioned Ronnie and liked what he heard and saw. Billy's other suggestion was a hairdresser called George Smith who had a good baritone voice. He too passed his audition with Alf. The concert party was complete and, after a period of intensive rehearsal, was ready for business.

Alf decided that if the expanded act was now a cohesive concert party, rather than just a bunch of disparate performers, they needed a collective name, so they all got together to discuss the matter. Ideas were tossed around, without much success, then the conversation drifted away from the matter in hand and on to the devastating air raids of the previous evening. Someone mentioned how the whole sky had spectacularly lit up over Coventry with multi-coloured 'Very Lights'. These were brightly coloured tracer flares, used to temporarily illuminate the night sky to give the anti-aircraft gunners a glimpse of their German aircraft targets. Their ungrammatical sounding name actually came from their American inventor, naval officer Edward Wilson Very. Billy picked up on the odd name and suggested their concert party could be called 'The Vary Lights', as they were a bright, colourful, varied gang, and the name would be easy to remember as everybody knew all about 'Very Lights', thanks to the ongoing Blitz. The others all liked the idea, with one small amendment. In order to make the name look trendy and quirky they used a deliberate misspelling – 'The Vary Lites'.

The Vary Lites were listed on club billings as: Alf Freeman (tenor), Freda (soprano), George (baritone), and Billy Breen (comedian), with Ronnie Hollis on piano. The line-up seems to have changed slightly over the years because later posters billed them as "The Four Vary Lites": Alf Freem (now shortened), Freda, Billy and George, with Alf Pack accompanying on piano, in place of Ronnie. They were all well-known locally in their own right, so bookings came flooding in.

Nell was always on the ball with what would work well in the act, and realised that George Smith's baritone would blend well with her daughter's soprano voice. Consequently, as well as performing his own solo spot, George sang beautiful romantic duets with Freda, which never left a dry eye in the house. Ronnie would pull the place down with his virtuoso piano numbers. His real show-stopper was belting out a rousing rendition of The Warsaw Concerto, whilst tap dancing at the same time. And Billy Breen brought a new highly successful and eye-catching dimension to his additional comedy spots in this longer show.

Billy had always enjoyed dressing up, and had discovered that he looked rather good in women's clothing, adding a new string to his bow as a female impersonator. This new departure was encouraged by 'Aunty Nell' Freeman. She'd take him round all the second hand clothes shops in nearby Coventry, and together they'd pick dresses which Nell would take home and adorn with sequins and bows. He didn't wear a wig, but when he pushed his thick wavy hair forward he said he looked just like Joan Crawford in *Autumn Leaves*. In drag he'd do impressions of his favourite Hollywood starlets, like Bette Davis and Katharine Hepburn. His big finish was "My Name is Tangerine", a steamy number, where he purred and growled like a sultry seductress, at a time when Eartha Kitt was still just a kitten.

Singing in drag and impersonating Hollywood starlets became an integral part of Billy Breen's act for almost twenty years, before he became Larry Grayson, doing the camp act wearing men's clothes which we all remember so fondly. As a solo drag act, after The Vary Lites years, he was sometimes billed as "Britain's Misleading Lady". I love the cleverness of the double meaning in his bill matter "Misleading Lady", but I feel sure, knowing of Larry's obsession with the cinema, that the neat soubriquet also passed more than a nod at the Claudette Colbert film of the same name, first released in 1932. Billy Breen in drag also became known as "the yes-yes girl, with the no-no eyes!", and "the reason the troops went east... and west..." because, towards the end of the war, he had become a regular on the forces entertainment circuit. The lads, appreciative of any entertaining break from the horrors and drudgery of war, would whistle, whoop and cheer at his female impersonations. For some of them it would be the nearest thing they'd seen to a real woman for quite some time.

The Vary Lites concert party proved very popular during the war. Often the air raid sirens would go off while they were on stage performing and the club concert secretary would make an announcement, giving the audience the option of going down the communal air raid shelters, or staying to watch the rest of The Vary Lites' show. Invariably people risked Hitler's bombs and stayed to the end. The morale boosting show was soon in demand in army camps, hospitals, factories, anti-aircraft sites, as well as all the biggest and best Midlands working men's clubs.

In the Industrial Midlands a lot of the men hadn't been called up to serve in the armed forces during the war because they worked in what were called 'reserved occupations'. These were jobs that were so important to the national war effort that any skilled workers or working men with vital experience were automatically exempt from being conscripted. In other words they were more valuable where they were than out in Europe fighting. In Coventry there were factories which made aeroplane engines, aircraft, vehicles and munitions, all of which were of great importance to a nation at war. Of course this is why the area was such a major and frequent target for cataclysmic German bombing raids.

Still only in his teens Billy helped the war effort by being a 'knocker-upper', which is not nearly as disreputable a job as it sounds. He basically was a human alarm clock. It was his job to be up at the crack of dawn, to wake the railway and factory workers, so that they weren't late for the early shift, which genuinely was vital for the war effort. He had to use a long pole to knock on the men's bedroom windows. There was a definite art to this because if you tapped a bit too enthusiastically you broke the glass, which didn't make you popular with big burly workmen. As Billy was now old enough to look after himself Fan was also able to do her bit for the war effort, and to add a little more to the household income, by getting a job in the canteen at one of the local factories.

As the war with Germany was just about to enter its third year William Sully White turned eighteen and received his call-up papers for National Service. Not too surprisingly, he failed his medical and was declared unfit for military service. There was mention of a weak heart, which surprised Billy. He'd always been sickly and had suffered many ailments, but it was the first and only time there was ever any suggestion of a weak heart. It seems likely that 'a weak heart' was a euphemism for Billy's effeminacy, which made him unsuitable for tough military training. Of course the doctor wasn't going to say it, but Billy's wrist was simply too limp to hold a rifle. Unlike America there was no actual rule banning homosexual men from the armed forces in Britain, but effeminate, camp or openly gay men were seen as a bit of an embarrassment, so their talents were put to good use elsewhere. I hasten to add that there were many gay war heroes, but they had to be very discreet about their sexuality in those intolerant times. Billy did his bit by entertaining the unfortunate locals who were constantly forced out of their homes and down the gloomy air raid shelters to escape the German bombardment. Morale boosters like young Billy Breen served their country in their own unique way, and helped keep the Great British indestructible spirit intact.

4

... a gay day... a tragic day... and a lost love...

This is probably as good a time as any to discuss 'the elephant in the room' – Billy / Larry's sexuality. He was always very discreet, in fact positively secretive, about his sexual orientation and steadfastly refused to discuss it. In the years of national fame Larry loved nothing more than pouring his heart out to journalists, columnists and interviewers, but the moment his sexuality was mentioned the shutters would come down. Asked why he'd never married he would trot out those old chestnuts about "never having found the right girl" and being "a confirmed bachelor". There was even a silly press story in 1977 about him planning to marry fifty-eight-year-old spinster Noele Gordon of 'Crossroads' fame, but that was never going to happen, despite their genuinely close friendship. In one press interview I have found, denying his and Noele's wedding plans, Larry went so far as to say: "Incidentally there's no reason why I shouldn't get married. Let me put it straight. I'm NOT strange in any way!"

The Gay Liberation Front were understandably at odds with him over those kind of statements. But it went further than that – they had a problem with Larry Grayson all together. They didn't like his caricature camp portrayal of a gay man for one thing, and they couldn't understand why he wouldn't be honest and 'come out of the closet'. It does seem odd in these more liberal times that he could make such capital on stage about being gay, and constantly make outrageously camp innuendoes, and yet fervently deny being gay in his real personal life. He never seemed to have the same problem with 'outing' his fictitious friend Everard! We mustn't forget however that

Billy was brought up, and was at his sexual peak, at a time when homosexual acts were still illegal in Britain, and the Hammond family were devout church-goers who wouldn't have approved of a same-sex liaison. There was a lot of pressure on him therefore to be secretive about his sexuality. Kenneth Williams, who had an aggressively homophobic father who was a strict Methodist chapel-goer, had a similar dilemma, and wrestled for years with the perceived morality of his sexual preferences. Many gay performers from that era felt they had to hide their sexuality as they believed 'coming out' would lose them all their fans and end their careers.

When I started doing the research for this book I half expected to find some secret male life partner that had been in a long-standing relationship with Billy / Larry. Many people of my generation grew up with Frankie Howerd always denying being gay, in the same way that Larry did, only to find that former waiter Dennis Heymer had been Frankie's secret live-in lover and partner for well over thirty years. I have found no such person in Larry's life. The truth is, apart from a couple of years just before he died, Billy / Larry lived with Fan all of his life, and she would not have approved of a resident lover, so there simply was no room for a live-in partner. From what I can learn there doesn't seem to have been any great desire to have a monogamous live-in lover either.

People who were close to Larry tend to close ranks and follow the party-line, presumably out of a commendable loyalty to Larry's memory. I have been told that he was almost asexual, having no interest whatsoever in intimacy with either gender. I don't think that is quite true either, however. It is a simple and effective way of ending any discussion on the matter, but is far too convenient to be the whole truth. Like everything in life I think it was much more complicated than that. With close associates, when the subject of sex came up, Larry would make a joke out of the fact that he couldn't be doing with all that "pushing and shoving". Taking the moral high ground he once told Terry Wogan on his eponymous chat show: "I can't bear all this getting into bed with everybody. It frightens my dog!" Perhaps the jokes hid some truth. He certainly was a bit of a prude about sexual matters, so maybe the physical act of sex really was abhorrent to him. However it is obvious that he found young men attractive, and there is absolutely no doubt that he actively sought and enjoyed the company of gay men, and loved to surround himself by equally camp male friends. That is a verifiable fact – anything beyond that has to be speculation or gossip.

Conversely though he never seemed to go to gay clubs or gay bars, or any other gay meeting places for that matter, much preferring to enjoy a nice cup of tea by the telly with Fan. He was in many ways a sexual enigma.

As I mentioned at the start of this book I had professional dealings with Larry myself, making a twenty-part series with him for BBC1 in 1988, so I got to know him reasonably well over a nine-month period, and I believe I had a good working relationship with him. In fact I became very fond of him. From that time there are a few cast-iron facts which I can personally vouch for regarding Larry. Firstly he never brought any hanger-on friends, gay or otherwise, with him to any of the many recording days at the BBC in Manchester. Larry was undoubtedly quite high maintenance, but Paul Vaughan, his manager, was always dutifully in attendance to look after him.

Another thing that I can say for certain is that Larry did develop a bit of a crush on me. I was prettier back then! I'll save the full story for a little later in the chronology of this book, but it was an unrequited crush as I was a happily-married heterosexual man with a toddler son. I never found it remotely uncomfortable or awkward, but he did get a little over-eager when he'd had a post-show gin and tonic, so Paul Vaughan kept him at a safe distance once Larry'd had a drink. I should point out though that this was far from the tried and tested seduction technique of an experienced Lothario; these were the almost comical naïve and clumsy advances of a teenage boy at the school prom. Bear in mind Larry was sixty-four by this point. I also saw him pin an anxious looking Tony Blackburn into the corner of the BBC Green Room after one of our recordings, in a similarly inept and equally unsuccessful seduction attempt. Truthfully Larry wasn't very good at holding his drink, and these amorous 'lunges' only ever happened after a gin and tonic. When he was stone cold sober he was no trouble at all. Even when he'd had a gin it wasn't a regular occurrence. Once Paul Vaughan had successfully steered Larry away from me I only ever saw him make advances to Tony Blackburn, and we had plenty of other good looking male guests on the series. Perhaps he had a thing for straight men called Tony! My reading of the situation was that Larry got a titillating thrill out of a bit of harmless flirtation with understanding heterosexual males, safe in the knowledge that his advances would be gently rebuffed, and nothing would come of it. Perhaps significantly nothing physical was going to be expected of him. I have a feeling that if I had acquiesced Larry would have run a mile.

I think Larry knew from a very early age, long before any thoughts about sexuality came along, that he wasn't like most of the other boys, and was a bit of an oddity. He once poignantly said to a journalist with a sigh and then a long chuckle: "Do you know sometimes I think I'm just a living walking breathing mistake!". When he hadn't had a drink I personally found him almost like a little old lady trapped in a man's body, which is possibly why he and Fan were always so close. Larry made me laugh a lot, and I almost felt like I was talking to a very funny maiden aunt when I spoke to him. I think he and Fan were probably two peas in a pod in all sorts of ways.

For anybody who realises they are different there are three ways you can continue with your life. One is to feel sorry for yourself, withdraw and crumble. The second way is to try to pretend that you are the same as everybody else, live a lie and risk being unhappy, frustrated and unfulfilled. But the best way forward, and certainly Larry's way, was to carve out an existence for yourself which suits and embraces your eccentricities, so you can enjoy life to the full. Vive la difference!

The only caveat to Larry's contentment with his life is supposition on my part, but perhaps he might have been happier if he'd been born in more enlightened times when he could have been open and honest about his sexuality. We will never know, but perhaps he would have enjoyed finding a man with whom to share his life. Maybe though he really didn't want that. He was certainly very happy living with Fan. But possibly it was the repression of society and his church-going family that prevented him from ever finding a 'significant other'. Larry always said he wouldn't have wanted to be born at any other time, but that was because he said he saw the last great days of British theatre, and the heyday of Hollywood and the silver screen. Maybe that was compensation enough for such a stage-struck young man, and finding a sexual partner to share his life with really wasn't that important to him.

One last thing I personally witnessed through working with him was the reaction of the fans, well some of them at least. A lot of the audience who loved his gossipy style were little old ladies who would hoot and cackle at every cheeky innuendo and camp gesture. However it is probably significant that I heard more than one of them say to me after the show: "Of course he's not really like that in real life, is he?... It's all an act..." That's obviously what they wanted to believe, hence the question being rhetorical. In fact I have probably never worked with anybody who has been more identical off stage and on. It wasn't an act really – what you saw was the real Larry Grayson. He *was* very camp and he *was* a gossip. A very funny one I hasten to add.

This brings us to his relationship with his close boyhood best friend, kindred spirit and soulmate Tom Proctor. Larry told Paul Vaughan that Tom was the one and only true love of his life. They met when they started school together at the age of five, so far too young to even consider sexual feelings, but they were clearly always like-minded and very similar in ways. They shared the same giggly sense of humour, they both loved the glamour of Hollywood and musical theatre, and they both had an equal hatred of sport, woodwork and anything that meant getting their hands dirty. They remained extremely close and shared a very special bond right up to Tom's tragic and untimely death.

During the war Tom managed to land a steady job at Herberts Tool Factory in Coventry, making munitions. This was one of those 'reserved occupations', vital to the war effort, so it looked like he would be exempt from National Service in the military. It seemed as though the two friends would both be spared the horrors of war. Cruelly and perversely it was Tom's lifelong inability to get out of bed in the morning that effectively led to him being killed. Billy had always joked that Tom would never get away with his tardy ways in the real adult world of work, and he was right. Tom received countless warnings about turning up late for his morning shift at the Herberts munitions factory. They even tried the extreme measure of laying him off, sending him to prison for two months for shirking his war effort, and then reinstating him in an attempt to shake him out of his lethargy, but that had no effect either. Tom still couldn't get to work on time. In the end the inevitable happened and he got the sack. The moment Tom was sacked his military call-up papers landed on the doorstep. Unlike his friend Billy he passed the medical for National Service with flying colours and he was put into the army for immediate and intensive training.

The first Billy knew about all this was one night when Tom turned up in the local pub wearing his brand new khaki army uniform. He was shocked to hear that his friend had been sacked from his reserved occupation, and was soon to be posted overseas to fight Hitler's hordes – something Tom seemed woefully ill-equipped for both physically and psychologically. Somehow they managed to make a joke out of the daunting prospect over a farewell drink. Billy said: "Well you'd better tell them that you don't mind going into battle providing it's not in the mornings!" and Tom countered with: "I've already thought of that, and I've asked to be put on the afternoon shift..."

That was the last joke they shared, and that was the last time they ever saw one another...

Billy's worst fears were realised with a shocking jolt one day in May 1944 when he picked up the local evening newspaper and saw a photograph of Tom on the front page, with the words: "Nuneaton soldier missing at Monte Cassino Italy". He had seen the cinema newsreels about the horrific battle at the Cassino Monastery which had been raging for weeks, but hadn't realised his friend Tom had been plunged right into the thick of it. Billy thoughtfully ran straight round to see Tom's mother, knowing she would be out of her mind with worry. She could see that Billy was as upset as she was and she tried to reassure her son's soulmate: "Tom'll be alright you know. I think he's been taken prisoner." Billy hoped beyond hope that she was right.

Sadly Mrs Proctor wasn't right. The awful news came through in a bone-chilling telegram a couple of weeks later – Tom Proctor had died of wounds received in active service at The Battle of Monte Cassino on May 3rd 1944. Tom's mother and five sisters were heartbroken, and so was Billy, who understood better than anybody just how terrified Tom must have been at the end. Billy had fretted about his sensitive friend being sent to the front line because he recalled that he and Tom had both been equally timid at school: "If anybody even fired a toy cap gun in the playground we would jump five feet in the air!".

Billy / Larry never forgot Tom Proctor. For the rest of his life he kept a yellowing newspaper cutting with a short 'In Memoriam' poem to Tom, which had been written by Tom's grieving sisters. He would take the poem out to read it on a regular basis, and always on Remembrance Day, every year. Paul Vaughan, who lives within the precincts of Worcester Cathedral, told me that right up to his own death, over fifty years later, Larry would often visit Worcester and go into the small peaceful war memorial chapel inside the High Altar of the cathedral to light a candle and have a few moments' silent and tearful contemplation in fond memory of his one lost love. He would also get his driver to take a detour off motorways, which he loathed, into small villages so that he could pop into the local parish church and quietly sit at the back, saying a silent prayer to his lost friend who had been so cruelly taken.

Billy and his loved ones had also had a very close call earlier in the war. As soon as the Coventry area had become a major target for German bombing raids the Hammonds had been forced to sleep in their own small air raid shelter at the bottom of the garden. When the bombing was particularly fierce Jim would round up Fan and Billy, and the Freemans next door and make them all sleep in the big communal shelter in the recreation field down the road. In the first week of April 1941 Jim sensed things were really hotting up and the Midlands was in for a very heavy bombardment. After a few days, on April 8th, he went round to see the Freemans and got everybody to move into the big shelter for the night. His instincts were spot-on because, when the all-clear was sounded the next morning, they returned home to find that both houses had taken a direct hit in the night, and were reduced to smouldering rubble, even their Anderson Shelters were flattened. Had Jim not moved them out to the bigger shelter they would have all been killed. They tried in vain to salvage a few bits and pieces from the debris, but all their possessions had either been crushed, shattered or ruined by the heavy rain that had fallen after the bomb had created its havoc. Both the Hammond and the Freeman family had lost everything, except the clothes they stood up in and a few bits and pieces they had taken down to the shelter. The Hammonds had even lost their pet dog, which was heartbreaking, as dogs weren't allowed down the shelters. However they had to be grateful to be alive themselves, unlike two hundred other people who were killed that night in the area and were later buried in a mass grave.

They all had to sleep in a school classroom for the next couple of weeks until the council could find them new housing in Friary Street. The first evening after the shocking devastation to their lives The Vary Lites had a booking to fulfil at a working men's club. They decided the show must go on, even though they had lost all their costumes and most of their props. After the show the concert secretary got up and told the audience what the Freemans and the Hammonds had endured the night before, and the personal losses they had sustained. The brave performers received a well-deserved standing ovation for their tenacity and their resilience.

When the Hammonds moved into their new home the council gave them coupons to get them started with basic utility furniture – tables, chairs, beds and so on, and slowly they managed to rebuild their lives, as many people had to do in those awful times. Billy though was most upset at losing his treasured collection of film magazines which he'd kept in mint condition for years, and were irreplaceable. He was also saddened to see that Holland's Fair had been hit by another bomb. The damage was beyond repair and they never opened again. They were all just collateral damage – an unfortunate consequence of living near a factory chimney, which had attracted the German bombers.

Thanks to these relentless raids the locals were forced down the communal air raid shelters on a regular basis. Billy made an important contribution to the community by keeping them smiling while they were cooped up down there.

When you think of Larry Grayson you can't help also thinking of his surreal cast of fictitious oddball friends and associates, like Everard, 'Slack Alice', 'Apricot Lil', 'Vinegar Vera', 'Self Raising Fred' the baker, and 'Pop It In Pete' the postman. Larry's gossipy stories of their outrageous exploits and shenanigans were a major part of his unique act and helped make him a star.

You may be surprised to learn that the vast majority of his bizarre coterie of cheekily named misfits and ne'er-do-wells were actually created as far back as those evenings entertaining in cold draughty air raid shelters during the war. Even more surprisingly some of those characters were based on real people who his captive audience must have all known. 'Apricot Lil' for example worked in the nearby Moorhouses jam factory on the apricot line; 'Vinegar Vera' worked in the neighbourhood chip shop; and 'Slack Alice' was the local coalman's daughter. Alice's prefix 'Slack' didn't refer to her morals, as many may have thought, but actually referred to her duties sweeping up the slack (coal crumbs) for her father, which was sold in different sacks from the best grade coal lumps. When times were hard in the Hammond household Billy would be sent round to sweet-talk Alice into giving him the odd sack of coal for the fire. She'd say: "I can't give you any coal, my dad would kill me, but I can let you have a bag of 'slack'." Billy thought it was such a funny word that he christened her 'Slack Alice', revelling in the double meaning. Her association with coal presumably explains why 'Slack Alice' was famous for her Black Bottom. Well she was in Billy's saucy stories about her.

Everard arrived on the scene a little later. Whilst on tour in the late 1950s Larry said he was staying in theatrical digs in Bradford, and got talking to the chatty landlady over a cup of tea and a piece of fairy cake. He was amused by the fact that, no matter how many times he corrected her, she insisted on calling him Mr Garrison. She then told Larry that she had a married daughter and an eleven-year-old son who was playing outside. Suddenly the back door opened and she yelled out: "Is that you our Everard?!", and in walked an odd looking mucky-kneed child with a football under his arm. He had long teeth, like a vampire, according to Larry. Larry said he remembered thinking: "He'll thank you for that name when he's eighteen!"

Larry found the unusual and enviably priapic moniker hilarious, so the name stuck with him as his fictitious close friend and confidante Everard Farquharson, who joined Slack Alice and the others in the act. Later still Larry would talk about Everard going everywhere with his close friend Michael Bonaventure. One cannot deny that his cast of imaginary characters were deliciously named.

Billy didn't really tell jokes, his style was much more intimate and anecdotal. He always claimed he couldn't even remember jokes. Previously there had been famous comics known as 'confidential comedians', but that was almost a euphemism for 'not very funny', so the similarity ends there, because he was hilarious. His style though was most definitely confidential. It was almost as though he was beckoning you to come closer so he could whisper "I shouldn't really be telling you this, but I'm going to anyway..."

Billy was developing the cheeky, slightly suggestive familiar Larry Grayson style, but he never crossed the line into being smutty, off-colour or crude. The Hammond household, which he adored and respected, was very church-going Christian, so there were clear boundaries to adhere to in his performances. Those principles stuck with him all the way through his performing career, something in which he prided himself. Fan would not approve of him being smutty. When he became a television star, constantly in need of new material, he would reject out of hand any scripts which he considered too near the knuckle. Larry knew instinctively where to draw the line. He called this intuitive self-censorship his 'amber light'. He might say something slightly saucy, made all the more outrageously risqué by a knowing look, but it remained family entertainment, because there was plenty for granny and the kids to enjoy, and they wouldn't latch on to the naughty innuendo, which made mum and dad howl so loudly with inexplicable laughter. It's a clever trick and few have perfected it.

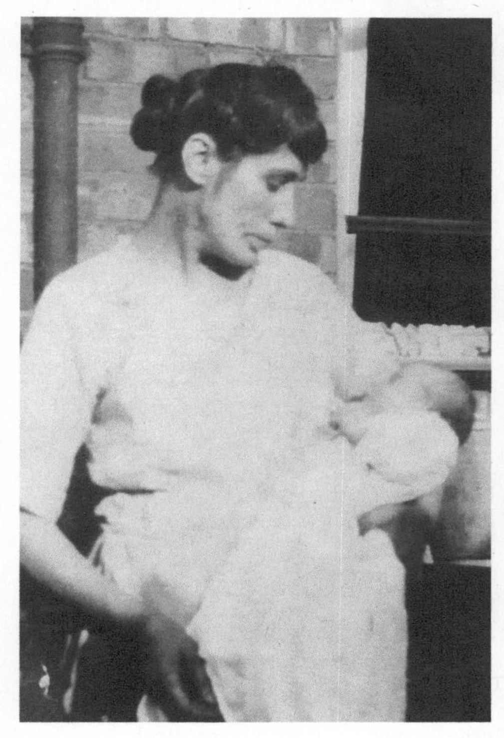

Top left: Baby Billy.
Top right: Ethel White, his mother.
Above left: Foster mother Alice Hammond and baby Billy.
Right: Foster father Jim Hammond and Billy.

Top left: Jim Hammond.

Top right: Foster sister Florence 'Fan' Hammond.

Above: Billy at Abbey Green Infants School.
Front row – the biggest smile if not the biggest hat.

Left: Billy actually driving, possibly for the first and last time in his life...

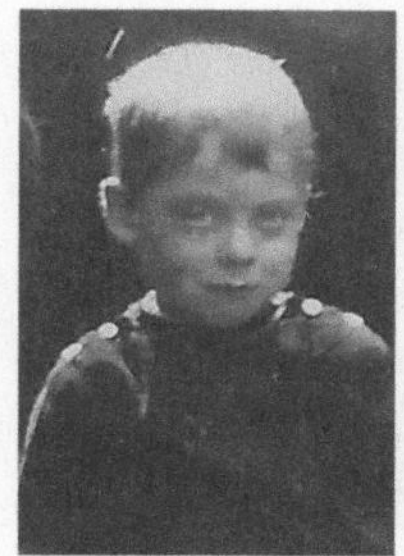

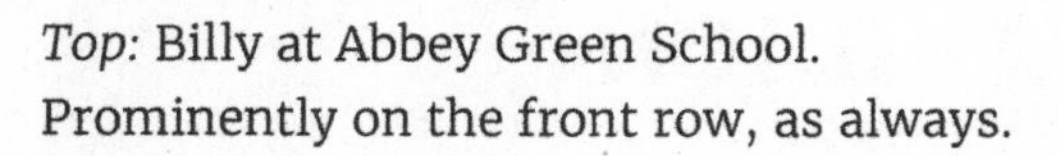

Top: Billy at Abbey Green School. Prominently on the front row, as always.

Above: Billy – the boy becomes a man... and a wannabe mean and moody matinee idol...

Right: Larry, aged 38, with real mum Ethel on the left, Fan and Jim on the right.

Left: Fife Street Working Men's Club in Nuneaton where Billy performed professionally for the first time.

Below: Billy with singer friend Alan Fenn, during *Radio Tymes* days.

NEW PAVILION
TELEPHONE 394 REDCAR Licensee—H. L. DODSWORTH

ALTERATION OF OPENING HOURS COMMENCING MAY 28th, 1951
MONDAY TO THURSDAY (INCLUSIVE) - ONCE NIGHTLY AT 7-30
FRIDAY AND SATURDAY - - - TWICE NIGHTLY AT 6 AND 8

BARRY WOOD presents

"RADIO TYMES"

A New Style Entertainment featuring artistes from the principal Radio & Television Programmes

TOMMY PACKHAM
RADIO'S NEWEST YOUNG COLOURED ENTERTAINER FROM BRITISH FORCES NETWORK

KEN MORRISTON
TELEVISION'S CONCERT ACCORDIONIST FROM "THE CENTRE SHOW"

TOMMY AUSTEN and ALAN FENN
RADIO LUXEMBOURG'S FAVOURITE MELODIANS TO SING FOR YOU MELODIES AND MEMORIES

JUDY REEVES
RADIO'S BRILLIANT TOP "C" SOPRANO

CELIA TUCKIE
DESIGN FOR DANCING

RON WALMER and LEONORA WHITELEY
TELEVISION'S NOVELTY MUSICAL, DANCING AND COMEDY ENTERTAINERS

BILLY BREEN
RADIO'S NEW YOUNG COMEDY GEM

FRED ATKINS

BARRY WOOD

STANLEY PICKARD
THE BROADCASTING PIANIST-COMPOSER

BILLY WINSOR and SYD WILTON

The Show produced, devised and compered by Barry Wood It's a Barry Wood Show ! ! !

ADMISSION – 2/6 1/9 1/3 1/- No Half-price
ADVANCE BOOKING OFFICE 10 a.m.–12 noon, 2 p.m.–4 p.m., 6-30 p.m.–7-30 p.m.

"Oh boy what a girl!" Britain's Misleading Lady.
The reason the troops went east... and west...

THE MAJESTIC,
SWADLINCOTE.

Resident Manager: J. S. AVERY

SUNDAY, APRIL 23rd, 1950, at 7-30 p.m.

BARRY WOOD presents

HUGHIE GREEN

OF B.B.C. FAME

IN

"OPPORTUNITY KNOCKS"

WITH

BILLY BREEN

THE MIDLAND'S FRANKIE HOWERD.

CLIFF GAY & IVY BARRY

IN MODERN COMEDY.

TOMMY AUSTIN & ALAN FENN

SINGING MELODIES
IN THE BOB AND ALF PEARSON MANNER.

BILLY KINTON

AT THE PIANO.

LOCAL DISCOVERIES.

Produced, Devised and Compered by Barry Wood.

Proceeds in aid of Church Gresley Memorial Hall Fund.

THEATRE ROYAL

LOUGHBOROUGH

Phone: 3774

WEEK COMMENCING MONDAY, JANUARY 21st, 1952

7-0 — ONCE NIGHTLY — 7-0

MATINEE SATURDAY AT 2-30 p.m.

THE POOLE ACADEMY

presents

A PANTOMIME FAIRY STORY

THE PIED PIPER

IN FOURTEEN SCENES.

MARGOT TURNER — PRINCIPAL GIRL
BILLY BREEN — DAME
PAULINE FARREN — PRINCIPAL BOY
PAT MILLIGAN
MEGAN GREASLEY — FAIRY QUEEN
ANGELA FOWLER — THE CRIPPLED BOY
PAMELA SAVORY — THE PIED PIPER
GWEN FARREN — SQUIRE
YVONNE BEXAN & ELINDA DARBY
AUDREY CHELL, JOY BROOKES, MARGARET DODGEON — THREE WISE COUNSELLORS

FAIRIES : GYPSIES : VILLAGERS : TROUPES : SPECIALITIES

PRICES OF ADMISSION :- Front Stalls & Front Circle 4/-
Centre Stalls & Upper Circle 2/9, Back Stalls 1/9 (Unreserved)

ENORMOUS ATTRACTION!!!

PALACE THEATRE

BATH LTD.

Telephone 2161

MONDAY, 30th NOVEMBER – For Two Weeks only

MONDAY TO FRIDAY 6.30 p.m. and 8.30 p.m.
SATURDAY ONLY 6 p.m. and 8.00 p.m.

BARRY WOOD personally presents

THE FAMOUS FAMILY ENTERTAINMENT

RADIO TYMES

with a star-studded cast of Radio and Television Artistes
with

BENNETT AND WILLIAMS
Those Radio Lads with their Phonofiddles
(Stars of more than 300 broadcasts)

GARY GRANDE AND DAVID MARS
The Merry Mirthful Mimers

BILLY BREEN
The Perfect Lady?

SYD CHESHIRE
The New Yorkshire Comedian

BILL GILMOUR
Radio's Romantic Baritone from "Kiss Me Kate"

COLIN ROBINS
The Popular Singing Impressionist

CLIFF GAY AND IVY BARRY
Television's Versatile Entertainers

FELOVIS
A Juggling Genius (Vide Press)

RON WAINMAN
Radio's Versatile Xylophonist

BRIAN SEYMOURS
The Personality Pianist

WALLY HILLIER
Music, Maestro Please!

DUDLEY DALE AND HIS GANG
of Boy Singers and Comedians

* IT'S A BARRY WOOD SHOW! *

BILLY BREEN

is one of the Midlands' most popular entertainers and hails from Nuneaton in Warwickshire. He commenced his professional career in Concert Party some seven years ago. His female impersonations have brought him considerable success and he has been with "Radio Tymes" for three years. Last season he played Dame in Pantomime when the Press heralded him as the youngest pantomime Dame in the country. He has a wide following with Tees-side audiences where he has earned for himself the title of the Northern Frankie Howerd.

Above: Billy's blurb from the *Radio Tymes* programme.

Opposite, top: Larry with The Honeys (Anita, Vilma and Pearl Liddell) and their mother.

MOSS'
HIPPODROME
Midland 2576/7
BIRMINGHAM
Manager & Licensee WILFRED MAY
Proprietors: MOSS' EMPIRES LTD.
Chairman: PRINCE LITTLER, C.B.E.
Managing Director: LESLIE A. MACDONNELL, O.B.E.
6.15 • MONDAY, OCTOBER 10TH • 8.30
BRITAIN'S NUMBER ONE RECORDING STAR
ADAM FAITH
HEAR HIS SMASH HITS
"WHEN JOHNNY COMES MARCHING HOME"
"POOR ME"
"WHAT DO YOU WANT"
JOHN BARRY SEVEN
JOAN & PAUL SHARRATT
"SO I WENT TO BED"
CHRIS CARLSEN
LARRY GRAYSON
HE'S PRICELESS
TELEVISION'S NEW VOCAL TRIO
THE HONEYS
COMPOSER OF "POOR ME" & "WHAT DO YOU WANT"
JOHNNY WORTH
ORIOLE RECORDING STAR

GAIETY BOX
REVUE 1968
Featuring the Great
of Femme Impersonators

AL BURNETT presents his 1970 hit show

"THE HA HA REVUE"

Starring America's No. 1 female impersonator

RICKY RENEE with Larry Grayson, Simon Smith

at 11.30 and 1.30 a.m. (Sun. 12.30 a.m.)

REGent 3686 | DINNER - SUPPER - BREAKFAST
DANCING TO 2 BANDS. OPEN SUNDAYS

JUNE 24th *For One Week Only*

THEATRE ROYAL - STRATFORD - E.15

Telephone: 534 8207

MONDAY – FRIDAY at 8 p.m. SATURDAY at 6.30 and 8.30 p.m

Stratford Entertainments Ltd. present

A CAMPING WE WILL GO

WITH

LANA

★ ★ ★ *PLUS ALL NEW STAR BILL WITH* ★ ★ ★

LARRY GRAYSON
TERRY DAY
DOUGIE BOUVIER
LEE STEVENS

Television's Opportunity Knocks 'MUSCLEMAN'
TONY HOLLAND

The Les Bien Girlies

Bertha Bent — Boner and Butch

Carmen Cottage — Chloe Kamp

In Stalls – DRINKS SERVED DURING SHOW

PRICES BOXES 20/- per seat STALLS TABLES 15/- 12/6 10/6
DRESS CIRCLE 15/- 12/6 10/6 UPPER CIRCLE 5/- 3/6 (unreserved)

BOOK NOW

Posters from Larry's critical transition years, on the cusp of fame. Not yet top of the bill, but beginning to get noticed in bigger and better shows.

He'll be doing better still in the next set of illustrations...

5

... making headway... a star of tomorrow...

Fan said the later war years, despite the grim realities, were a very happy time for her, Billy and their 'dad'. They made a lot of friends from the American troops who came over to Britain. They'd come round with rationed or hard-to-come-by treats like tobacco and coffee. Billy was living the dream as an entertainer, and they had recovered from the trauma of losing their home in the bombing raids.

Once the war was over a lot of the young men who had been called up for National Service started returning to the Midlands, demobbed from their various military units. Not only were they rejoicing about victory over Germany, they were also celebrating still being alive. There was a party atmosphere and the clubs and pubs were all packed, so popular acts like The Vary Lites were in big demand.

The teenage Billy Breen had spent a few years finding his feet as an entertainer, but gaining invaluable experience in the process. He was still trying to work out the best way to exploit his admittedly limited talents, so, in those early days, he preferred to seek the security of working with other performers. As well as appearing with The Vary Lites he formed a double act with a comedian called Ken Daniels. Daniels & Breen lasted a couple of years, and then he tried another stage partnership with a singer called Hazel Cook, which came to an abrupt halt when she got married and emigrated to Canada. In the end he realised his natural comedic skills and charismatic stage presence were all he needed, so Billy Breen became a solo act. He started out doing a few extra nights a week as a solo entertainer in the Midlands clubs, whilst still appearing with The Vary Lites at weekends.

The austerity of the post-war 1940s made for a grey dull Britain, which went on well into the 1950s. Ordinary working people sought glamour through entertainment, so Billy's female impersonations were always well received. With this evolution of his performance Billy had discovered a clever way of almost doubling his appearance fee. A working men's club would book him to perform two very different acts. He would arrive at the club early, to allow himself plenty of time to make himself up and look his best in a short frock and a beret. Britain's Misleading Lady would then make her big entrance, carrying a sling handbag, with the crowd-pleasing opening line: "I've just returned from Portsmouth!". Presumably this got a big laugh because Portsmouth had gained a bit of a reputation for its ladies of the night, hanging around the dock to entertain the sailors.

Billy would do a few songs and monologues in drag, something which always seemed to go down well in working class places of entertainment, then the club's concert secretary would announce that the pies had arrived, or there would be a couple of cards of bingo. This would allow him an interval to quickly wipe off the make-up, take off the glamorous frock and beret, and slip on a lounge suit and tie to return on stage for the second half of the show as Mr Billy Breen, camp comedian and raconteur. Most people in the audience didn't even realise that the two acts were one and the same person, so everybody was happy. The audience got two apparently different variety acts, the club only had to deal with one performer, Billy got two fees, and Fan got to put more away in his Post Office savings account.

By 1946 the post-war partying and victory celebrations were over, and life in Britain was returning to normal. Billy was still enjoying working with Uncle Alf and The Vary Lites. He was making a good steady living with them too, but he was twenty-three and wanting to spread his wings. He had all the confidence and ambition of youth, not to mention a yearning to do a bit more with his life.

The next small step up the tall showbusiness ladder, and the true breakthrough for Billy Breen as a full-time solo performer, was once again thanks to his showbiz guardian angels, the Freeman family. They had a theatrical friend called Harry Leslie, who was a real old pro. Harry had made a name for himself playing pantomime dame. More importantly though he had become an impresario who put together small scale variety and revue tours which went round the smaller villages and remote country towns that didn't get the big shows, and weren't part of the major variety circuits in those days. If Harry ever had a spare week he would come to Nuneaton to stay with his friends, the Freeman family. One such week was Christmas 1946. He mentioned to Alf and Nell that he was planning to take a variety revue on tour around the West Country and wondered if they knew any suitable local acts that he could take a look at. They of course told him all about their young protégé Billy Breen. Harry, a dapper little man in his fifties with a high reedy voice, thought the lad sounded ideal and asked if he could meet him. Billy was duly summoned and sang his signature song "In The Bushes at the Bottom of the Garden", with Freda accompanying him on the piano. Mr Leslie was impressed enough to ask if he could see more, and went along to watch The Vary Lites perform in Coventry a few days later. He enjoyed their performance so much he not only offered Billy a place in his new show, but he also hired their tap dancing pianist Ronnie Hollis, and Harry even persuaded Alf Freeman to leave his butcher's shop in the hands of his capable staff and come on tour as well. Billy was thrilled by this amazing opportunity, and must have been pleased that there would always be a couple of familiar and friendly faces around on this big new adventure, to give him moral support.

Harry Leslie's revue, which toured Devon and Cornwall in the early months of 1947, was prophetically called *Tomorrow's Stars*. The big-time was still a long way off for Billy Breen, but this was definitely a step in the right direction, and it meant playing small theatres and village halls, a step up in gentility and sophistication from the working men's clubs of the industrial Midlands.

Alf Freeman was the only one who had a car, so he drove them all down to Devon, with their props and costumes following behind in a tow-trailer he had borrowed. It was one of the worst winters in living memory and the arduous journey south was a nightmare, hitting snow drift after snow drift. There were no motorways back then, so the journey would have taken a long time, even in fair weather conditions. Worse still cars didn't have heaters in those days. It's a wonder they didn't all succumb to hypothermia. Eventually they reached Kenton in North Devon, the starting point for the tour. Fortunately Harry Leslie had the foresight to book all the accommodation in advance, so they were soon thawing their frozen bones by a log fire in a cosy cottage which was to be home for the first couple of days.

The deal was that Harry would pay for their bed and breakfast accommodation, plus any other meals, and they would each be paid the princely sum of two pounds a week, which gave them just about enough to buy a few drinks and send a little bit home.

There were just seven of them in the company. The line-up was: Harry Leslie himself, who did a bit of everything; Brenda Gaye, who sang soprano; a very loud trumpet player and comic turn called Roy Mercer; Ronnie Hollis bizarrely tap dancing at the piano; singing his beautiful baritone ballads was Alf Freeman, who had shortened his stage name to 'Alf Freem' to sound more American; then there was drag act and comedian Billy Breen of course; and, last but not least, there was Johnny Fanthom, "Ace accordionist and the fastest fingers in captivity". They each had a solo spot in the show, but they were all expected to appear in the production numbers and sketches to give the impression of a cast of thousands... Well, more than seven anyway...

Mr Leslie insisted that the entire company appear in the big opening number, with all the men in smart suits. It meant that Billy had to perfect a very quick change to make his grand entrance in drag, to perform his first solo song, just a short time later. There was no Velcro in those days, and no dresser to help – both of which facilitated some impressive quick changes that Larry did in later shows, to great effect. His record was a quick change he and his dresser perfected twice-nightly during the run of *Grayson's Scandals* where he would close the show and leave the stage in a grey suit and black shoes, and reappear fifteen seconds later in a white suit and white shoes to do an encore.

The drastic gender transformation in *Tomorrow's Stars* never failed to get a gasp from the audience. Most of the simple post-war working West Country folk had never seen a man dressed as a woman before, and it was something of a shock at first. For Billy it couldn't have worked better. Every performer needs to grab the attention of their audience within the first few vital moments of their act, or they run the risk of never impressing them, and 'dying a death'. Billy had them all by the scruffs of their necks with astonishment right from the word go, then his charm and charisma would win them over, making him a memorable hit everywhere the show went.

Larry said that during that opening ensemble number Harry Leslie could count the heads in the audience and calculate what they'd taken at the box office that evening, whilst he was still singing. He was always correct to the very last penny.

During those cold winter months of early 1947 Harry Leslie taught Billy a lot about the practicalities of theatrical touring, generously sharing his years of personal experience, right down to the best way to pack your props and costumes. They only played two nights in each new village or small town, so they were constantly 'getting in' and 'getting out' of all the very different church halls and small venues, which was hard work. The troupe's 'fit up', as it was known, even involved putting up their own curtains in many of the halls, and lifting heavy pianos up on to the stage or platform. All the hard physical work and long hours were worth it though because the audiences were so appreciative, not being used to getting such professional entertainment coming to them. Harry Leslie was very exacting about every aspect of the show, so Billy learned a lot from him professionally as well. "You came on far too early last night Billy – watch Roy and see how he does it." Harry Leslie even insisted that the entire company went to which ever was the nearest church every Sunday so that the locals would see that the visiting theatricals were 'respectable'.

Because of the bad weather they often had to elicit the help of local farmers with their tractors to help them deal with all the snow and ice, but one way or another they always managed to turn up at the next venue on time. They did good business too. *Tomorrow's Stars* were probably the high spot of that entire bleak winter for many of the folk living in those remote country areas. The only village where attendances were poor was Monkokehampton near Hatherleigh. It's not clear why Harry Leslie kept returning because he said business was always terrible there. He told Billy: "You could put on 'The Last Supper', with the original cast, and you still wouldn't fill the place!"

The only downside of touring for young Billy, and this applied right throughout his career, was being away from home. He loved being at home with Fan, and he would always get home after a show if humanly possible. He missed Fan when he had to be away on tour, and she missed him. She hated not knowing where he was, and she worried about him, because she knew how much he liked his home comforts. She also knew how fussy he was about food, so she worried whether he was getting enough to eat. Fan said he always phoned her every single night when he was working away, and talked for ages. She didn't like having to put the phone down. The best thing she said was hearing how excited he was when he had gone down well in a big venue he'd never played before, but she always knew he was homesick deep down, even though he rarely admitted it.

When he became one of Britain's most popular entertainers Larry Grayson said that, whilst he had always dreamed of being a famous star, he never felt bitter or frustrated in the early days, and always thoroughly enjoyed every phase of his entertainment career, no matter where he was in the pecking order of showbusiness success. He loved his time with Harry Leslie's *Tomorrow's Stars*, despite the damp beds of the cheap theatrical digs, and the paucity of money. It seems, from every interview that Larry ever gave, and everything he said to friends and family, that he was always comfortable in his own unique skin, and enjoyed life to the full, appreciating everything that happened to him. If only more of us could be so content.

The highly successful *Tomorrow's Stars* tour lasted for three months, after which Billy returned to Nuneaton and went back to work around the Midlands club circuit. The other club acts, who were all now his circle of friends, thought he'd been mad touring tiny country villages in such terrible weather for just two pounds a week, but Billy had learned so much from Harry Leslie and the other experienced performers that he knew it had been the right thing to do. He was returning to the working men's clubs with lots of new improved material, a fresh approach to his whole act, and bigger and better goals to aim for in showbusiness. The only thing was the word 'tomorrow' in *Tomorrow's Stars* had perhaps been a bit optimistic. He was still over twenty years away from being a star.

During World War II Harry Leslie had created possibly Britain's first boy band called 'The Four Blue Pages', a music and singing act. There were many members over the years, with Harry refreshing the line-up periodically with all the young new talent he found. Billy Breen, despite his limitations in the vocal department, was one of many faces who appeared as one of 'The Four Blue Pages', which allowed him to work for Harry Leslie again in the early 1950s. There was no cross-dressing in this act, so Billy had to wear the uniform blazer and slacks, but he couldn't resist the temptation to crowbar some comedy into the ostensibly serious musical act.

Billy / Larry was always a firm believer in the guiding hand of fate. He believed that everything is mapped out for you, in some massive book of life, before you are born. Perhaps it is understandable, when you look at the extraordinary way in which his own life and career panned out, but personally I think you make your own good fortune, and I also think he was particularly good at that. Of course most success stories also have an element of luck about them. You have to be in the right place at the right time, and there are often coincidental occurrences and events which play into your hands. In Billy's case a good example is the Freeman family moving in next door just as he was about to leave school. However you still have to know how to grab those opportunities with both hands and how to use them to your best advantage.

His firmly held belief in fate and guardian angels led to a lifelong interest in fortune telling and clairvoyance. The first time Billy ever went to have somebody 'read' his future was in April 1950, by an eccentric old-fashioned woman called Poll Thomson. He believed that he'd been led to her by fate itself. Poll was a stereotypical fortune teller with grisly taxidermy around her dimly-lit home, pot dog ornaments, evocative photos of wounded soldiers, and a thick tasselled tablecloth on the 'reading table', where she gazed into the bottom of an old china teacup to see the future written in the remaining tea leaves and dregs. Fortunately teabags hadn't yet become fashionable, or she would have been lost. Billy had gone with a female friend called April who had the first reading. It was all the usual vague stuff about going on a journey, somebody in the family getting married next year, and her having to be careful about somebody with 'M' in their name, but Billy was fascinated. He sat transfixed, listening to all Poll's predictions for April. Of course then he wanted to take his turn in the hotseat. Out came the tarot cards and Poll interpreted their meaning for the agog Billy. She said that she saw him climbing stairs, and crossing water, and she could tell that he hadn't been well. She was unsurprisingly one hundred per cent accurate so far, which meant Billy was hooked and was hanging on her every word. Poll told him that in the near future he would be working near water, which would start a new and very happy period of his life. She then tantalisingly foretold from his tea leaves that one day he would be at the very top of his chosen profession, but she said that rise to fame won't start "until there is a seven".

Of course all these cryptic predictions are deliberately vague so that you can put your own interpretation on them and convince yourself that they were accurate. A few years later Billy felt that 1957 had been a good year, which meant, in his eyes at least, that Poll had been right. The truth is that he would have also given her the credit if something good had happened five years earlier on July 7th 1952. In fact when he finally broke through as a star in 1970 Larry decided that must be the seven to which Poll was referring. If she'd really seen 1957 or 1970 as significant why didn't she just say 1957 or 1970?

In my view telling a touring entertainer that they may be going to work at some point near water is a fairly safe bet as well, especially when you think how many theatres and performing venues are near lakes, rivers, canals and the sea. However Billy truly believed that his next rung up the steep showbusiness ladder was accurately foretold by Poll Thomson. Whether Poll had foreseen it or not, it was definitely a very positive step in the right direction.

A few weeks after the tarot card reading there was an unexpected knock on the door one Sunday evening...

6

... Radio Tymes are happy times... and provide the origins of a catchphrase...

When the all-important knock on the door came Fan was sewing and Billy was reading so, thinking it was just one of the neighbours popping round, Billy didn't bother to get up and yelled "Come in!". The door opened and in strode a big middle-aged man with a broken nose and the physique of an all-in wrestling champion. He was wearing an expensive Crombie coat and a long bright yellow scarf. It wasn't of course a neighbour, but Billy recognised him immediately from seeing his photograph in *The Stage* newspaper. "Are you Billy Breen?" the man asked. "Yes, and you are Barry Wood aren't you?" he replied. It was only then that Billy noticed the smaller younger man walking behind, in the big man's shadow. Barry Wood was a well-known theatre impresario. The smaller man with him was called Alan Fenn, a local up-and-coming young singer who Billy knew from the club circuit, and became a very close friend. Apparently Alan had told Barry all about this very funny comedian from Nuneaton. Barry trusted Alan Fenn's judgment so implicitly that he offered Billy a job right there and then on the spot, without auditioning him, or even going to see him work: "sight unseen".

Barry was producing a touring version of the seminal radio talent show *Opportunity Knocks* (which later moved to TV), hosted on stage by its creator Hughie Green. They were coming to The Majestic Cinema in nearby Swadlincote, South Derbyshire, and had a spare slot to fill. Barry Wood invited Billy to appear in the first half of the show, which featured established local acts as a prelude to Hughie's amateur discoveries in the second half.

Wood was so impressed by his 'blind booking' that he wrote to Billy a week later inviting him to join a forthcoming variety spectacular summer season production, called *Radio Tymes*, for a six-week run at The Pier Pavilion Theatre in South Shields, on the north east coast of England, not far from Newcastle. Of course, because this was a seaside pier theatre booking, Billy said it proved that Poll Thomson's prediction that he would be "working near water" was about to come true.

Billy had to do his own solo act, as well as joining in the production numbers and the sketches, just like his busy but enjoyable time with Harry Leslie. He was also told that "an ability to work in drag would be an advantage". Of course that was meat and drink to Billy Breen in those days. In fact his name appeared in the souvenir programme, followed by the billing: "The sultry siren of Shields. Oh boy, what a girl!".

His fee was to be twelve pounds a week, and the contract stipulated that he was required to dress well on stage and off, and he must conduct himself "in a manner befitting the Company". Barry Wood, or 'Mother' as the acts all called him, liked to think of himself as a strict taskmaster. He did demand one hundred per cent effort and professionalism from his performers, but Billy couldn't take the strictness too seriously. He was always playing tricks on Barry, and teasing him. Despite his stocky build Barry Wood was very camp and would break into a profuse sweat when Billy teased him, and out would come a large powder puff to dab down the shine. Also, just like at school, Billy was constantly in trouble for chattering when Barry was trying to get the company's attention.

The six-week run was a huge success – so much so that on the final Monday Barry Wood bustled into the theatre and called everybody together. Billy was gossiping as usual and had to be told to shut his mouth for five minutes if he wanted to hear some good news. An impresario called Ernest Binns had seen their show and wanted to book it for a further two weeks at The New Pavilion Theatre in another nearby north east coast seaside resort, Redcar. This was a prestigious booking so Barry told everybody to pull out all the stops when they got there.

The cast did indeed pull out all the stops, and they did very good business in Redcar. On the last night of the extra two weeks they performed a special finale with a tear-jerking rendition of "We'll Meet Again", followed by an emotional farewell speech from Barry Wood. Tearful but happy the performers thought that was the end of the road, but were surprised when

The Mayor of Redcar mounted the stage, wearing his chains of office. Billy thought it must be a presentation to Barry or a thank you to the cast, but it was better than that. The Mayor made a short speech praising the production and its "grand bunch of artists", before adding: "And now ladies and gentlemen I have a nice surprise for you all. Mister Barry Wood and his *Radio Tymes* Company have been booked for the entire summer season in this theatre next year!". This was wonderful news for Billy and the rest of the cast, who could relax in the knowledge that they had a long summer season coming up the following year, with guaranteed quality work for eighteen weeks in a prestigious venue. In fact *Radio Tymes* was so successful that they played for several consecutive summer seasons in The New Pavilion Theatre in Redcar, with Billy Breen in the cast for five years, from 1951 onwards. The New Pavilion was known as 'the glasshouse' by the locals, because of its all-glass roof. It was a medium-sized theatre, seating around eight hundred people, so Billy was definitely moving up in the world.

In an effort to boost the nation's morale the summer of 1951 was known as 'The Festival of Britain', so Barry created a big patriotic opening number called: "All The World is Coming to Redcar in 1951". 'All the world' may have been a slight exaggeration, but the people of Redcar and environs loved it. Billy thought it was hilarious, but he didn't dare snigger in front of the boss.

Barry Wood, aka 'Mother', was obviously a real theatrical character. He always compered the shows he produced, and even insisted on singing the odd song. He liked to think he was a bit of a Noël Coward type, with one hand suavely tucked in his jacket pocket as he crooned, which must have looked somewhat incongruous with his broken nose and his wrestler's physique. He also had trouble hitting the high notes. As Billy said at the time: "He murders songs, but he knows how to put together a good show, and that's the main thing."

Barry Wood was true to his contractual word about how the cast must conduct themselves "in a manner befitting the Company". He didn't like them fraternising with the locals and would intervene if he found they were dating people from Redcar. It was as though he had eyes in the back of his head. He reprimanded one young male performer for being seen eating out in restaurants with a local girl, and having an afternoon out with her in nearby Stockton-on-Tees. He even ticked Billy off for chatting to two local lads outside the stage door during a show. He ordered Billy to get back inside and told him from that day on the stage door would be locked during performances. Of course he couldn't actually go through with his threat because it would have contravened fire regulations, but it shows how determined he was to stop the performers mixing with the general public. Having said that, Barry didn't allow the cast to date one another either. He seemed, rather unreasonably, to want all his healthy young good-looking company to live a monastic life of celibacy while they were working for him. Presumably he was terrified of the slightest whiff of scandal that might jeopardise ticket sales, or maybe he was just rather possessive about his 'gang'.

Barry knew nothing about the cinema, being so besotted by all things theatrical, so Billy could easily wind him up by saying things like: "There will be nobody in the theatre tonight Barry because Cecil B De Mille has just released a massive Technicolor epic and they will all be queuing round the block for cinema seats..." Out would come the powder puff again, dabbing the nervous sweat away. He fell for Billy's teasing every time.

Billy got away with things other members of the company would never have risked. He'd play tricks on other acts like telling them that Barry had cancelled their spot in the first half, as the show was overrunning, then he'd giggle as their music played and they missed their cue because they were reading in their dressing room. He'd shout out when the impressionist was on: "Nothing like him!" That sort of unprofessional mischief wouldn't usually be tolerated in a professional theatre company. 'Mother' would feign anger, then threaten to sack Billy and send him home on the next train, but Billy would just dramatically flounce out, clasping his forehead, saying: "You may say that in a crowded room to impress people, but I'll bet you're glad you've got me!" Billy's relationship with his older boss seems almost flirtatious, with all the teasing, followed by Barry's ineffectual reprimands. One cannot help be reminded of the coquettish precocious sixth form schoolgirl teasing her somewhat flustered middle-aged geography master.

Barry did change the acts occasionally – bringing in new performers to refresh the show, and to encourage repeat business from the locals, so there were plenty of opportunities to get rid of Billy if he'd really wanted to. However, despite the frisson of tension between them, or quite possibly because of it, one constant in the show was Billy Breen.

A large proportion of their audience were locals who would come back time and time again, so the company would have to come up with new sketches and new ideas every week so that there was always something the regulars had never seen before. This was a bit of a bone of contention with trouble-maker Billy because the posters and the programmes all said *Radio Tymes* was devised and produced by Barry Wood. Billy complained that they did all the devising while Barry sat back and took all the credit. On the plus side their ingenuity, local in-jokes and re-invention for the people of Redcar made them the toast of the town. Their loyal fans would literally queue round the block every time the show was revamped. Parties were thrown for them, gifts would be given, and they were made feel welcome everywhere they went. In that small pond they were very big fish indeed.

During his later successful years Larry got his driver to take him on a nostalgic pilgrimage back to Redcar. He was shocked how much it had changed, and not for the better. Sadly it was no longer the seaside resort of his fond memories. In fact he remembered his summers in Redcar so fondly that Larry left a sum of money to the local RNLI lifeboatmen in his will, several of whom turned up at his memorial service in London to pay their respects.

Barry Wood would open the show by welcoming the audience to the show which boasts: "a star-studded cast of radio and television artistes". Then he'd say: "Will you sit back in your seats ladies and gentlemen and enjoy two hours fast and furious, as we turn over the pages of these *Radio Tymes...*" Of course the title of the show was calculated to make people think of broadcasting stars, as the *Radio Times* was the only listings magazine in those days and, as such, had a massive circulation. Wood had shrewdly changed the spelling to 'Tymes' to avoid copyright issues with the BBC. The truth was that not one single member of the company had ever appeared on radio or television, but that didn't stop Barry from introducing their solo spots as "direct from The Forces Network", or "that brilliant broadcasting entertainer from BBC radio's *Workers Playtime...*" Of course the audience believed every word, and half of them even thought they remembered hearing the broadcast. Billy Breen appeared on one poster as "Radio's new young comedy gem", even though he'd never appeared on radio. One act Barry would introduce as "the stars of over two thousand broadcasts on Radio Burma and Radio India". They too had never appeared on radio, not even once.

In a strange but hilarious boast in *The Performer*, a variety theatre newspaper, Barry Wood took out an ad' saying that his hit family entertainment show had a star-studded cast of twenty-two artistes, with "No nudes or passengers".

It is said that Larry's most famous catchphrase arrived on the scene during that first full summer season of *Radio Tymes* in 1951. The stage of The New Pavilion was notoriously draughty, as the theatre was exposed to the elements, being right on the seafront promenade. A side door was often left open and a bracing North Sea wind would whistle right across the stage. Billy would look off into the wings with disdain and call out in an arch voice to some unseen stagehand: "Shut that door!"

In showbiz lore there are of course several very different anecdotal versions of where that iconic catchphrase came from. I even saw some *Guardian* reader pontificating that Larry's "Shut that door" was in fact a consciously Anglicised bastardisation of the French phrase "Je t'adore", meaning "I love you", but I feel, as Captain Mainwaring might well have said to Corporal Jones: "I think you're entering the realms of fantasy there..." Another often repeated story was that Evelyn 'Evie' Taylor, Larry's agent / manager in the late fifties and early sixties, used to sweep into his dressing-room with the latest piece of salacious gossip, or something confidential to discuss, beckoning Larry and insisting, with a conspiratorial whisper, "I've got something to tell you. Shut that door!", a phrase he then repeated on stage as an affectionate mocking of his agent. The Redcar story predates that one by nearly ten years though. I personally favour the Redcar version. It is more logical as he often followed the much-mimicked catchphrase with the words: "The draught in 'ere is wicked!", and the intonation was always slightly exasperated as though it was being repeated to some indolent stagehand in the wings, who had already ignored the instruction a couple of times. Of course Evie Taylor may well have picked up on his already tried and tested catchphrase and used it to dramatic effect when she wanted privacy. Anyway, take your pick. I'm guessing Larry himself probably forgot where it really came from.

Incidentally Larry's other equally famous catchphrase "What a gay day!" actually started life as "Well I've had a freak week!", which didn't catch on. The moment he changed it to "What a gay day!" the audience roared with laughter. They always say that audiences create catchphrases, not comedians. The evolution of these verbal trademarks is fascinating. Perhaps Tommy Cooper spent two years saying: "A bit like this!", before he stumbled upon "Just like that!" At a time when the word 'gay' was more usually used to mean joyful and carefree, the double meaning when Larry used the word in such a camp manner was still appreciated. Comedy is often like a conspiracy between the audience and the performer. "I know that you know that what I am saying can be taken two ways... and you know that I know which way I really mean it..."

Although I can understand why some gay men found Larry offensive I can also appreciate that he was being quite daring really when he said: "What a gay day!". He was openly saying: "I am what I am". One could argue that the audiences' approval was a positive thing, and opened a door for more acceptance for the gay community in a previously intolerant world.

Larry's catchphrase "Look at the muck on 'ere!" had more mundane origins. He was performing in a really dirty old theatre, covered in cobwebs and dust. He ran his finger along one of the props, looking genuinely aghast, and commented on the muck, getting a huge laugh from the audience in the process. From that day it remained in the act.

The summer season of 1951 was a very happy time for Billy Breen, and indeed for the whole *Radio Tymes* company, so there were a lot of tears on the final night as the last notes of "We'll Meet Again" faded away. Of course they did meet again because Barry Wood was invited to stage the show once more in the same theatre the following summer as it had been such a massive success. After the last show the company all exchanged kisses, hugs and gifts. None of the cast could afford cars so they had to get all their trunks full of costumes and personal effects home on the train. The thoughtful and kind thing therefore was to buy your fellow performers a small but memorable end-of-season gift which would pack easily. Billy hadn't really liked one of the girls in the show so he bought her a large wooden clothes horse, knowing full well that she would struggle with it on her long journey home, which involved two station changes.

Being in a hit show like *Radio Tymes* did Billy no harm at all, and the success of their consecutive summer seasons in Redcar led to Barry Wood booking him as a support act in other small scale provincial tours of the production, which were preferable to the tough club work he'd previously been accustomed to. Despite their occasional tiffs Barry knew when he was on to a good thing.

In between the 1951 summer season and the 1952 summer season of *Radio Tymes* in Redcar Billy Breen was amicably released from his contract with Barry Wood to appear at The Theatre Royal in Loughborough in his first ever professional pantomime, something he enjoyed immensely. He got plenty of 'copy' in the local papers by saying at just twenty-eight years of age he was probably the youngest pantomime dame in the business.

It was a rarely performed panto – *The Pied Piper* – but it still had all the traditional bewildering elements, including the Principal Boy and the Principal Girl both being played by leggy girls and becoming lovers, not to mention the Dame being played by a man. In fact this production had a particularly confusing slant to its casting as all the male parts were played by women, including: the Pied Piper himself, the Squire, the Principal Boy, 'Hans', 'Tim and Tough', the three wise counsellors and 'the crippled boy'. Being an established female impersonator Billy Breen was of course ideal for the role of Dame Winkler. He had such long thick wavy hair in those days he didn't even have to wear a wig for the part. According to the poster, Billy was the only male member of the entire cast, and yet he was playing one of the very few female parts. The kids in the audience must have found it even more baffling than the average pantomime.

The panto was well received, and an ever more confident and optimistic Billy Breen returned to the Barry Wood fold in good time for the 1952 summer season of *Radio Tymes* in Redcar.

In the theatre programmes for *Radio Tymes* Barry Wood had a penchant for using excruciating puns. In the 1951 programme, after the name Billy Breen appears, there are the cringe-worthy words: "To give you the time of your laugh". The following year it simply said: "Billy Breen – Gay's the word!". Now it's hard to know whether that was a sly wink and a nod to Larry's sexuality, although he never described himself as gay, and seemed to dislike the word used in that way, so the sixty-five year old description of Billy is possibly the now archaic use of the word 'gay' to mean happy, joyous and carefree. I somehow doubt the double meaning was a complete coincidence, however.

Barry and Billy, who had started merely as business associates, became great friends during this productive time together, and had a lot of mutual respect for one another. Wood might not have had much of a singing voice, but he did have a good eye for up-and-coming talent. After a couple of years in Redcar he had other versions of *Radio Tymes* in other northern seaside resorts, using different acts, but Barry continued to sign Billy Breen to be in the Redcar cast for a further three years, five summer seasons in total. Other rising stars, like The Dallas Boys, appeared in different incarnations of Barry Wood's *Radio Tymes* in the fifties, but it was Billy who made a real name for himself and looked destined for imminent fame and fortune.

7

... Billy Breen is discovered... and Larry Grayson is born...

Billy Breen was still a popular name in the Midlands working men's clubs, and that's where he always returned between more sedate theatrical bookings. When it came to club work Billy rarely needed to venture outside the thriving pub and club circuit of the Midlands, however he did make a rare guest appearance 'down south' in June 1956 at The Nuffield Club (aka The Nuffield Centre), in central London, near Trafalgar Square. This hugely popular services club, which finally closed its doors in 1980, provided cheap food in its huge canteen; cut-price drinks; games rooms for darts, dominoes, billiards and table tennis; plus free live entertainment for forces personnel on leave, war veterans and ex-servicemen and women. Twice-weekly quality variety shows were staged every Tuesday and Friday, with an orchestra performing every Sunday evening. These free shows were made possible by the fact that the club was non-profit-making and none of the magnanimous artistes or musicians received a fee for their performances.

Despite the lack of a fee up-and-coming variety acts were always keen to perform at The Nuffield Centre as many of the top London showbiz agents popped in on Tuesdays and Fridays, scouting for new talent. A lady he only ever knew as Mrs Cook booked the acts, but a friend of Billy's had put in a good word and recommended him to her. Mrs Cook duly booked Billy for a Tuesday evening show, which didn't interfere too much with his busy weekend schedule back home. There were a lot of acts on the bill that night, so it was chaotic backstage and cramped dressing rooms had to be shared. With so many acts on the bill it was important to make yourself stand out so

Billy gave it everything he'd got when it came to his turn. He came off stage, in his own words, "sweating like a dray horse". Another comedy performer hurriedly fought his way into the crowded dressing-room towards Billy. He was a small man called Rex Jameson who famously performed in drag as 'Mrs Shufflewick', in a similarly sexless frumpy style to Norman Evans, 'Old Mother Riley', and more recently 'Mrs Brown'. Rex told the perspiring Billy: "Get your make-up off quick because I want you to meet someone who has been watching you."

This was exciting news for Billy, so he quickly mopped his brow, smartened himself up, and went out into the corridor where a strikingly elegant blonde woman in a blue dress and a blue hat was patiently waiting for him. The blonde lady said: "Hello love. I've been watching you and I'm very impressed. My name is Evie Taylor. I think your timing is marvellous – you are a very funny boy..." Evie gave Billy her business card and told him to come to her office the following morning at eleven o'clock. He looked at the card in almost disbelief. Evelyn, or Evie Taylor was an agent with The Will Collins Agency, who were based in Chandos Place, right in the heart of London's theatreland. Joseph William Collins was a big agent at the time and known as a star-maker. In fact he quite literally made two stars of his own – his internationally successful daughters Jackie Collins and Dame Joan Collins. As an agent he had discovered a teenage Shirley Bassey and had guided the early careers of Peter Sellers and Harry Secombe. Billy couldn't believe it. His first appearance at The Nuffield Centre and he had been discovered by a major London agent.

Thrilled to be even getting in through the door of one of the West End's biggest and most prestigious agencies Billy Breen presented himself smartly and promptly the next morning for his appointment with Evie Taylor. She made him feel welcome and gave him a seat, then got straight to business: "The first thing we have to do is change your name. I don't like Billy Breen – it's got to go..." Billy, who hadn't expected anything more than possibly a couple of trial London bookings, realised she was taking him under her wing and preparing to sign him up, so he was sensible enough to agree right away to her demands: "Yes Miss Taylor".

Evie said she didn't like his existing stage name because it was too mundane. She said he needed something more memorable and glamorous sounding. They struggled with this conundrum for quite some time. Names, inspired by Billy's lifelong love of The Golden Age of Hollywood, were tossed around and then rejected for one reason or another. In the end Billy suggested 'Grayson', as an homage to one of his favourite Hollywood musical idols, Kathryn Grayson (star of 'Kiss Me Kate'). Evie's eyes lit up at last. She liked the sound of Grayson, but what would make a suitable first name? Billy Grayson, the most obvious choice, was immediately rejected by Evie. She offered several better alternatives: Bobby Grayson, then Leslie, then Lennie, before settling on 'Larry'. She made Billy write it down to see how it looked. Larry Grayson. They both agreed it looked just perfect. She quickly snatched up the phone to her boss: "Hello Mr Collins. I've got Larry Grayson here – Yes, that funny boy I told you about from The Nuffield Centre. I'll bring him straight down..."

The new-born thirty-two-year-old Larry Grayson was positively overwhelmed as he was ushered into the great man's office. Will Collins, or 'Joe' to his friends, put him at his ease by saying what great things he had heard about him from Evie. Larry's jaw must have just about hit the floor as Joe went on to thrillingly say that he had already lined up four weeks of engagements for Larry to fulfil – the first week at The Dudley Hippodrome; followed by a week at The Palace Theatre in Skegness; then a week at The Regal Cinema in Great Yarmouth; plus a week at The Regal Cinema in St Leonards-on-Sea. At a time when cinemas were staging top variety shows these were all good quality high-status bookings. Larry was then given the card of a top London showbusiness tailor called Firman, who would make him a new suit just like those worn by Joe and Evie's already successful clients Mike and Bernie Winters. He was also instructed to present himself a few days later at the famous Landseer Studios to have a new publicity photograph taken in his new stage suit. Larry Grayson could hardly believe how fast things were happening.

He had only been inside The Will Collins Agency offices for an hour, but it turned out to be a life-changing hour. William Sully White walked out of that imposing building sixty minutes later, floating on cloud nine, with a new London agent; a proper personal manager and guardian angel in the form of Evie Taylor; four prestigious new bookings; and a new well-groomed look... not to mention a new moniker which would eventually become a household name. Evie's parting words said it all. She told him that they were going to bill Larry Grayson as "He's priceless"... Adding, to his delight: "Because you are..."

Three weeks later, on Monday July 16th 1956, Larry arrived at the first of the four venues, The Dudley Hippodrome. True to Evie's promise he was greeted by a poster which trumpeted "Carroll Levis and his discoveries" at the top of the bill, supported by: "Larry Grayson – He's priceless!". Dudley was so close to Nuneaton he was able to travel by double-decker bus. Chauffeur-driven limos were still way off in the future, but for Larry this already was beginning to feel like his childhood dream of stardom come true. He later said he felt like he was in a trance that day.

Evie Taylor had stayed in London, but she phoned Larry in the stage door office after the first house on that opening Monday night. She told him that she had already spoken to the theatre manager who had told her that Larry had been marvellous in the first house, and, if the rest of the week went just as well, then her new signing was on his way to becoming a star. His attentive manager then checked that Larry was happy with his play-on music, the band's backing for his song, and his dressing room, before gently reminding him to make the most of this important engagement and not waste a single moment of his ten-minute spot. When he anxiously said that the famous talent scout Carroll Levis hadn't yet spoken to him, Evie reassured him by saying that was a good sign – it meant Levis was jealous that Larry was better than his own discoveries. With that ego-soothing compliment Evie wished him luck with his second house and hung up with her usual endearing sign-off: "Bye love!"

If anything the second house went even better than the first house, which was absolutely thrilling for Larry because, with The Dudley Hippodrome being so close to home, his beloved foster father Jim Hammond, along with his foster sisters Fan and May, plus a gang of old friends had come to the second house to support him, and witness the inaugural night of Larry Grayson. Jim Hammond must have been the proudest dad in the world. For the first time in his eighteen-year career Larry had a dressing room large enough to entertain his enthusiastic and excited supporters and loved ones after the show. In clubs he'd often had to change in the backstage lavatory. This really was beginning to feel like being a star. His diary entry for that night read: "Tonight Larry Grayson walked out on to the stage for the very first time. I think he will do well."

The rest of the week was a triumph, with more friends coming along to see him and to cheer him on. The Palace Theatre in Skegness was a little further from home, but no less of a success. However it was the third of the four weeks which was to be especially significant to Larry. It was the week at The Regal Cinema in Great Yarmouth, where he was supporting the top of the bill, another big star from the Joe Collins stable, singer Dorothy Squires. No less than 'The King', Elvis Presley himself, once said that she was his favourite singer. Dorothy was known as Britain's Judy Garland, and was every bit as big a gay icon. Larry adored her, so it was a thrill just to meet her, never mind to share a stage with her.

Just before the opening night in Yarmouth the stage manager came to Larry's dressing room with an exciting personal message from Dorothy Squires. She wanted Larry to introduce her show-stopping closing spot, which he of course saw as a great honour. Worried about what to say Larry was told to go to the great lady's dressing room to discuss her introduction. He knocked nervously on the star dressing room door and found himself face to face with Dorothy's husband – Roger Moore, who was then an up-and-coming young television actor. Larry was quite overcome as Miss Squires called out to invite him in. They got on well, with Roger Moore sitting listening, "the strong silent type" as Larry described him, while his wife put Larry at his ease and happily agreed upon the wording of his suggested stage introduction. He was rather touched that, after the show, Dorothy sent Roger Moore to Larry's dressing-room with an envelope containing a generous cash gratuity as a thank you for his gracious and kind words of introduction.

Dorothy and Larry had a joyous week together, with Larry still in awe of this diva superstar and gay icon. On the last day Larry received another phone call from Evie Taylor with more good news. Dorothy Squires had called her to say that her new protégé was marvellous, and she wanted him to appear on stage with her again in three weeks time when she was due to play a week at The Chiswick Empire in London. Of course Larry was over the moon.

After the first show, on the Monday night in Chiswick, Larry heard Dorothy call from outside his dressing room: "You're getting stuck up aren't you? You haven't been in to say 'hello'...". He thought it wasn't his place to go knocking on a superstar's door, as she might be busy, but she told him that was nonsense and insisted he come along to her dressing room right away for a drink with her and Roger. They chatted away about the theatre and Dorothy's tours around the world, and began a friendship which was to endure.

At the end of that week, during a tearful farewell, Dorothy assured Larry that one day he would be a star, because he was such a funny boy. Praise couldn't have come from a higher source in his eyes, and he was deeply touched by her kind words, even though real stardom still seemed out of reach for Larry. In a gratifying bit of serendipity or showbiz karma, the real breakthrough came for Larry Grayson when he stole the show on television sixteen years later, with Dorothy Squires topping the bill on "Saturday Variety". As he came off stage that night Dorothy flung her arms around him, and with genuine tears of joy in her eyes, she said: "I always told you that you would be a star one day!".

Signing with Evie Taylor and Joe at The Will Collins Agency was an enormous boost to Larry's confidence and self-esteem. He found himself playing all the major variety theatres, and touring with some of the country's biggest stars. It must have seemed like the classic rise to mid twentieth century stardom, following a similar career pattern to the likes of Bruce Forsyth, Morecambe & Wise, Tommy Cooper, Peter Sellers, Harry Secombe, Tony Hancock, and many other household names. They had all started as young men, entertaining the troops. They then served their apprenticeships at the bottom of the bill, learning their craft, and perfecting their material, progressing to bigger and more prestigious venues, better productions, and rising higher up the bill. In the 1950s the next stepping stone to becoming a big star was a guest spot or two on radio or, better still, television. Unfortunately this is where Larry Grayson had his first set-back, and lost pace with his fast rising contemporaries.

He must have thought his big break had come a little later in 1956 when his new manager Evie Taylor told him that top BBC comedy broadcaster Kenneth Horne, most famous for his ground-breaking 1960s radio show *Round the Horne*, had invited Larry to appear on a television comedy special he was hosting, called *Opening Night.* Like all shows in those days *Opening Night* was transmitted live, and Larry Grayson's high camp performance caused consternation and outrage in middle England, with the chattering classes all lunging for the 'off' button in their droves. Homophobic viewers' letters poured into the BBC complaining that they didn't want to see "that sort of person" on their television sets ever again.

It is interesting that the working class audiences in the seaside theatres and country village halls had all embraced Billy Breen's performances as family entertainment. Even in the predominantly all-male notoriously rough tough working men's clubs around Nuneaton Billy Breen had been welcomed, liked and appreciated as a wholesome act. Camp homosexuality has never seemed a problem to the aristocracy, so it was most definitely the middle classes who had a blind spot for Larry's comedic style, and indeed his overt sexuality. Outraged of Tunbridge Wells strikes again. The BBC had to listen to this very vocal bigoted minority of their licence-payers however. Larry Grayson was simply too camp for television, or so it appeared in those less enlightened days. Larry must have thought that would be his first and last ever appearance on the increasingly important medium of television.

Larry licked his wounds from this bruising experience and resigned himself to the fact that stardom was probably never going to come his way. It must have been a heart-breaking blow, but he bounced back and still continued to enjoy doing what he was good at, and appearing where he was welcome. So he knuckled under and returned to a constantly busy schedule of variety theatre work, supporting bigger and more famous acts for his mentor Evie Taylor.

It now looked like Larry would never be rich, but he was continuing to earn a good steady living, and he had bought a small terraced house for himself, Fan and foster father Jim in his beloved Nuneaton – number 52 Clifton Road. With a fitted bathroom, an indoor lavatory, and a washing machine, it was a definite improvement on the Abbey Green house where the Hammonds had brought him up. This humble but happy house remained his home until he found fame in the 1970s. He was even reluctant to leave Clifton Road then, but his manager at the time persuaded him that a big star couldn't possibly live in a terraced house in a working class area.

Larry loved living in Clifton Road. He and Fan got on well with all the neighbours and, because he was working hard and making relatively good money, number 52 was one of the very few houses with a telephone. It was an essential requirement for a busy performer with an agent in London. Ever-canny Fan put a money box by the phone and allowed the neighbours to make calls for tuppence a time. Larry loved this arrangement because the walls of number 52 were pretty thin and he could hear the loudly whispered gossipy conversations about doctor's appointments, ill health, disreputable friends and relations, and juicy scandal, giving him more and more material for the blossoming act that we all remember so well. He particularly liked all the many malapropisms they would come out with, and he would scribble them down on the back of a fag packet for use on stage at some later date. He heard one woman describing a recipe that needed a spoonful of dislocated coconut; another that was extolling the virtues of perforated coffee; yet another who was excited by her forthcoming coach trip to see The Blackpool Hallucinations; a lady who had seen a show where the star got a standing ovulation at the end; and a woman who was excusing her mistakes by saying that nobody is inflammable. One neighbour barged in wanting to use the phone, realised it was a bad moment, and said: "Oh, I'm sorry for protruding!". Who needs scriptwriters with neighbours like that?

Unfortunately, on top of his hurtful BBC debacle, there was another insidiously growing threat to Larry's career. Just as he had finally clawed his way into the much coveted world of the 'number one' variety theatre circuit, he realised it was a world that was about to become extinct. It must have seemed a cruel irony that television, the medium which had so callously rejected him, was the very thing which was tolling the death knell for variety theatre. People found they could see all the big stars on television, so they became more and more reluctant to leave their warm homes and comfortable armchairs to pay good money to see the same acts in theatres. As ticket sales plummeted, so the budgets for the shows were reduced and the productions became less lavish, leaving paying audiences disappointed and less likely to return to the theatre another time. This self-perpetuating downward spiral inevitably led to the closure of many theatres, and was eventually to spell the end for this once popular and lucrative form of British entertainment.

Out of desperation several theatrical impresarios had resorted to staging 'nudie shows'. This awkward mix of static female nudity in tableau form, punctuated by variety acts, was presumably inspired by Vivian Van Damm's unlikely success at The Windmill Theatre in Soho with *Revudeville*, "the show which never clothed". On tour though this sort of seedy entertainment didn't appeal to the mums, and the dads didn't dare admit it appealed to them either. Not only that but many of the top acts refused to lower themselves to appear in these shows, so the quality of the productions was never going to be great. Family audiences stayed at home in front of the new cosy television set, and the downward spiral continued unabated.

Evie Taylor was nobody's fool and could see the writing on the wall for variety theatre, so she was moving more and more towards the new entertainment craze – pop music and rock 'n' roll. She left the Will Collins Agency and started up on her own, taking her comedy discovery Larry Grayson with her. Ultimately Evie became even more famous and successful for setting up her own personal management company to look after and nurture some of Britain's biggest pop stars of the late fifties and early 1960s.

Evie spotted a good looking charismatic nineteen year old singer called Terry Nelhams in 1959. Literally taking a leaf from The Garden of Eden Eve renamed her creation Adam. 'Adam Faith', with his mop of blonde hair and finely chiselled looks, became an overnight pop sensation and teen heart-throb. Then in 1964 Evie signed up seventeen year old newcomer Sandie Shaw, who had a number one hit with her second ever single. In fact it was Evie Taylor who persuaded Sandie Shaw, against her better judgment, to sing the 1967 British entry in The Eurovision Song Contest. Evie's unerring showbiz instincts were absolutely right though – Sandie's song "Puppet On A String" was one of the very few wins for the United Kingdom.

Just like the 'nudie shows' other gimmicks were tried in an attempt to breathe life back into the dying world of variety theatre. In the early 1960s there was a peculiar and rather uneasy fusion of the embryonic but rapidly emerging pop music phenomenon with the old world of variety. Pop music mogul Don Arden, father of Sharon Osbourne, is credited with this peculiar innovation, born out of the uncomfortable truth that pop stars were great box office, and the appeal of variety performers was waning. For example, in 1963, Kenny Lynch, Helen Shapiro and Irish stand-up comedian Dave Allen were all part of a variety bill on The Beatles' first full scale national theatre tour. For a few years these shows were successful, but, by the mid-sixties, huge and influential acts like The Beatles decided this uncomfortable marriage was 'uncool' and had to end. The superfluous variety acts were unceremoniously dropped from future pop and rock tours. Nevertheless during the honeymoon period Evie Taylor, thanks largely to Adam Faith's pulling power with young screaming audiences, could still fill theatres. This meant that she was able to send Larry Grayson out as a rather unlikely support act with Adam Faith around all the Moss Empire Theatres, which had of course been the number one touring circuit in its heyday. Larry, who was still billed as "He's priceless" on the Adam Faith posters, loved playing this legendary theatre circuit, even though it meant being away from Fan and Nuneaton more than he liked. This major national tour spanned 1960 – 1961.

It's not clear whether it was Evie Taylor's influence that stopped Larry doing the female impersonations, but it seems more than a coincidence that the drag part of his act was dropped at the same time as the name Billy Breen. I'm sure Ms Taylor would not have put Larry on tour with wholesome teen heart-throb Adam Faith if he'd still been a drag act. Other than as a pantomime dame Larry never did appear in public in drag again but, interestingly, Paul Vaughan, his last manager, told me that Larry kept just one of his performance dresses in his wardrobe right up until the day he died, presumably as a fond reminder of an important part of his life.

Sadly the inexorable theatre closures were escalating daily, and the latter part of the Adam Faith tour was relegated to large cinemas, which were also struggling to find people-pleasing gimmicks in a vain attempt to compete with the ever-more powerful medium of television. Cinemas were being turned into bingo halls; theatres were being pulled down or turned into supermarkets. It was a depressing time for variety performers. One such comedy star, who was still trying to cling on to the tail end of a stratospheric touring theatre career was the legendary Jimmy James. He too found himself as a support act on the later Adam Faith dates. It must have been a come-down for a veteran comedian who had been at the very top of the tree, headlining in all the major British theatres, to find himself a warm-up act for a teenage audience who neither knew nor cared who he was and had only come to scream at a pop singer's blonde quiff and dimpled chin. Nevertheless Jimmy James kept his dignity and did the shows with good grace and his usual consummate professionalism. Larry was in awe of such a famous old pro and was very flattered when Jimmy invited him into his dressing room one night for a cup of tea. Incidentally Jimmy James was famous for playing a very funny drunk, but in real life he was completely teetotal, being a slave not to the bottle, but to his ever-present teapot. Jimmy had been watching Larry's act and, like Dorothy Squires before him, assured Larry that he had the makings of a star. There is no doubt it was good for his ego to keep getting these compliments from his stage idols, but it didn't seem to be getting him anywhere.

Adam Faith was definitely the goose that laid the golden eggs as far as Evie Taylor was concerned, so she would often turn up at various venues on the tour to keep an eye on the show. She had been on the stage herself for many years, so she knew instinctively what was working and what wasn't. She had in fact been a singer with a unique gimmick in her act – she beat time with a pair of cymbals strapped to her knees. She was no shrinking violet either, so she wasn't afraid of telling her clients if something wasn't exactly right. Larry said you could always tell whether you were in her good books or her bad books by the way she addressed you backstage. If she just used your first name that meant she was in a good mood with you, but if she shouted "Larry Grayson – where are you?" you knew you were in trouble. Even the star of the show wasn't immune from her sharp tongue. When her admonishments weren't aimed at you they could be positively hilarious. Larry recalled her raising her voice after the show one night, saying: "Adam Faith! What do you think you are doing? I was sitting in the third row of the stalls tonight, and when you hit that last note five people in front of me got up to leave for Russia!" Any man will probably agree that you don't argue with a woman who can play the cymbals between her knees.

Larry never complained about Evie Taylor, in fact he got on extremely well with her, and respected her hugely, but she did have a fearsome reputation. She would harangue and yell at theatre managers if things weren't just to her liking for her clients. In the end both Adam Faith and Sandie Shaw openly criticised Evie and parted acrimoniously from her business clutches, saying she was "emotionally violent". They said she would often threaten to end their careers if they did not accept her terms and demands.

Larry's parting with Evie came before that public slanging match however, and appears to have been much more amicable. In the early sixties she was concentrating more and more on her stable of pop stars, and musicians like John Barry, the composer and musician, probably most famous for his long musical association with the James Bond movie franchise. With the variety circuit on its knees she had less and less to offer Larry in the way of work, so, between theatre appearances, he had been doing the odd club booking back in the Midlands. The club concert secretaries however were getting tired of him asking for work when it suited him, and then cancelling club bookings if a better offer came along from Evie Taylor. He was delivered an ultimatum – he was either available for club work or he wasn't. Having to accept the unpalatable truth that variety theatre was rapidly becoming a thing of the past, Larry reluctantly told Evie that he was in danger of losing his valuable connections with the working men's club circuit, so he would no longer be able to accept theatre tours. It must have been a tough decision to make, and an even tougher conversation to have with Evie Taylor, his guardian angel who had tried so hard to turn him into a star. This parting of the ways was probably almost a relief to Evie, who could no longer guarantee her 'very funny boy' the work she felt he deserved.

Content as a successful, but not famous performer, Billy Breen / Larry Grayson had grafted his way through the 1950s and early 1960s, constantly working, but never top of the bill. He'd packed out the local clubs where he was well-known and much-loved, and he'd played all the big theatres, supporting the big stars of the day, but his own national stardom now seemed an impossible dream.

Larry always said he wouldn't have missed that long period when his name was so small on the bill, because it would have meant not meeting so many wonderful people. However, as he passed his fortieth birthday in 1963, for the first time he began to lose his undying childhood belief that one day he would be a star. It was a heartbreaking realisation. He felt he had to accept the fact that it was now too late and he would never be top of the bill, which meant that his name, Billy Breen or Larry Grayson, would sadly never be up in lights. Many of his contemporaries had already made it, or they had disappeared into obscurity. Stardom happened to younger people, and The Swinging Sixties was a time when the spotlight was firmly on youth. The new comedy stars were made on television – sparky youngsters like Liverpudlian newcomer Jimmy Tarbuck, who shot to fame at the age of just twenty-four, when he took over as regular host and compere of the iconic ITV show *Sunday Night at the London Palladium* in 1964. The mid-to-late sixties was the first truly dark time in Larry's otherwise happy career. Sadly it wouldn't be the last...

8

... a backward step... a bleak prospect... and a dark time...

Larry Grayson's dark period began in 1963 when he had to cope with the death of his real mother Ethel White. She was sixty-nine. Ethel had come to stay with Larry and Fan at Clifton Road. Her employer Mr Bray, who had kept a roof over her head while she was his housekeeper, had long since died, so she had been living with her younger sister Winifred ('Wynne') for quite some time. Finally, in his fortieth year, Larry saw an opportunity to live under the same roof as his real mother for the first time since he was nine weeks old. He jumped at the chance and hoped she would make Clifton Road her new home. Ethel had told Larry and Fan when she moved in: "Oh I've come to stay a long time", which of course pleased Larry enormously, but sadly it wasn't to be. After just three days Larry took her an early morning cup of tea up to her bedroom and found that she had died peacefully in her sleep. It was a very traumatic experience for Larry, and totally unexpected. She hadn't even finished unpacking all her things, so tragically devoted mother and son never did get to live together.

On the day that Ethel passed away Larry had a booking to do a show that evening at The Smethwick Working Men's Club. After giving it some thought he decided he had to turn up and do the show as if everything was normal, even though he didn't feel like going on and being funny. But he said that's how his mother would have wished it. He confided in the other performers who were appearing that night, telling them all about the awful experience of finding his mother dead in bed that morning. They of course told him he should go home, but he insisted that the show must go on.

Poignantly, in his third and final spot that night, Larry had to close by singing "When You're Smiling". Larry said: "How I got through it I don't know. The audience didn't know my sorrow, but then I looked to the wings and all the rest of the performers were there watching me. It was their love that got me through. When it was all over I just broke down and cried."

A fellow entertainer and long time friend, a banjo player who just went by the name of 'Ena', rushed to his dressing room afterwards to find him crying like his heart would break. Ena helped him pack his case and somehow got him home.

In the following days Larry said the overwhelming grief at losing his mother made him feel terrible – nervous and on edge. He claimed that the ghost of his late mother appeared one night, standing at the foot of his bed, saying she was quite alright and very happy in the afterlife, then she smiled at him and disappeared again. Larry said he stopped grieving so badly once she had told him she was okay. Ethel had always been bemused by her son's extroverted desire to be up on stage in front of hundreds of people, and couldn't really understand it as she was so introverted and quiet herself. She was of course terribly proud of him nonetheless, and Larry always said it was a great personal sadness that neither she, nor his foster mum Alice, lived to see him become really successful and famous.

Larry told a newspaper journalist in the mid seventies: "My real mother could never understand how I came to be on the stage. Those were the days when I was roughing it, and she laughed about that. One of the saddest things is that she died before seeing me become a star. She would have liked that. But it didn't happen for me until 1972. That's a terrible regret."

The only high spot in the mid-sixties for an increasingly depressed Larry Grayson was the opportunity to meet his all-time idol Judy Garland. She was, and still is, probably the most famous gay icon of all time. The coy euphemism "friend of Dorothy", describing a gay man, of course derives from her iconic performance as Dorothy Gale in *The Wizard of Oz.* I once saw her referred to as the Elvis Presley for gay men. Larry had been obsessed with Ms Garland since he first saw her up there on the silver screen in 1938 in a film called *Everybody Sing.* He immediately became besotted by her, collecting photographs, cuttings, and of course all of her records. He became a devoted member of The Judy Garland Club, a fan club dedicated to the great lady, which was formed in 1963. The club was endorsed by Judy herself, so, because it had her blessing and approval, she would liaise with the club organisers and invite club members to recording sessions, first night parties and backstage get-togethers. In 1965 she was in Britain for a series of cabaret engagements, so she happily agreed to attend a Judy Garland Club afternoon tea in The Woburn Room at The Russell Hotel in central London. Larry of course just had to be there.

Judy usually chose to stay at The Russell Hotel when she was in London and fans, including Larry, would congregate outside the front door if they had heard she was in town, in the hope of catching a glimpse of their idol. It was something very special then to be invited inside to meet the great lady in person.

Larry said the atmosphere was positively electric just before four o'clock, the time she was due to arrive. Promptly, and without any announcement, the door burst open and in swept Judy Garland, the great diva, in person. The place of course went into uproar. She asked the nearest man to take her coat, which was then passed to Larry. He stood there like a lovesick puppy clutching his idol's coat. She was dressed plainly in a grey woollen dress, but she couldn't have got a bigger reaction if she been wearing spun gold and finest silk. Eventually calm prevailed and everybody settled down. She chatted and answered questions posed by her adoring fans. Larry couldn't take his eyes off her, but he was almost glad she didn't talk to him personally, as he said he wouldn't have been able to speak. He said he was completely choked with emotion just by being in his Hollywood heroine's presence. The club organisers then screened her 1946 film *The Harvey Girls*, which she talked all the way through, making everybody laugh with personal reminiscences and gossipy insights into the making of the movie. She had only promised to stay for one hour, but she didn't actually leave until twenty past seven, so presumably she enjoyed meeting her British worshippers. Before she left she asked if they'd like her to sing a song. Silly question! By the end of her exclusive fan club rendition of "Make Someone Happy" there literally wasn't a dry eye in the house. Larry's last glimpse of Judy Garland was her waving at them all from the back seat of her limo as she was driven away. He knew that would probably be the closest he would ever get to her. Sadly she died just four years later, before Larry was a big enough star to meet her properly on a more equal footing.

He was devastated by her untimely death in 1969 and said: "It was as though part of my life had gone." Upon her tragic death Larry elevated her to the status of one of his guardian angels. Michael Grade told me that after a particularly good show in the famous years Larry would look up to heaven and say: "She's up there Michael. Judy's watching over me." He adopted some of her famously flamboyant gestures and mannerisms, knowing what a great performer she was. Michael Grade said even Larry's sign-off "I love you very much" was inspired by his guardian angel Judy Garland. Larry's familiar play-on music, which became his signature tune, was "The Man That Got Away", the song famously sung by Judy in her classic movie *A Star Is Born*. He even named his house after her when he became famous and bought a bigger place. Larry was much more than just a fan – he was obsessed by Judy Garland.

After the joyous experience of meeting his all-time idol it was back to the harsh realities of his own unhappy life for Larry Grayson. In the mid-to-late sixties Larry had two debilitating bouts of serious illness quite close together, both caused by peptic ulcers, the first it seems brought on by worry over his foster father's failing health. Tragically in 1966 Jim Hammond had to have a leg amputated, at the age of eighty-six, which was an understandably upsetting time for Larry and Fan. Jim had suffered a foot injury in an accident down the coalmines when he was much younger and still working, and a bad fracture had never been set properly. It left him with a limp for the rest of his life. In his later years it had affected his circulation and gave him a lot of pain and discomfort. One night he was in such terrible pain that they had to take him to hospital, where the doctors decided the only course of action was to amputate the whole leg.

Jim was eventually sent home, wheelchair bound for what was left of his life. Larry took his dad out for some fresh air, pushing his wheelchair round the local park, when he himself had terrible pains in his abdomen. As soon as they got home Larry collapsed on the floor and an ambulance whisked him into hospital where they gave him a blood transfusion. His peptic stomach ulcers, brought on by stress and depression, had haemorrhaged.

Larry had an awful lot to cope with around that time, not least all his worries about work, and the depressing realisation that stardom was probably now never going to come. Just as he'd finally broken into the lucrative variety circuit he'd had to stand by and watch as theatres closed every day, forced out of business by the burgeoning power of television, a medium in which he felt unwanted and unwelcome. He had been forced to leave his manager and guardian angel Evie Taylor, who could no longer secure him the prestigious theatre bookings she had previously been able to guarantee him in the now defunct Moss Empire circuit. Larry, through no fault of his own, had been forced to take a dispiriting step backwards, returning to the dingy smoky clubs and pubs of the Midlands. Previously every new step had been a step up the showbusiness ladder, but this was quite the opposite. His once promising career had hit a depressingly low ebb.

Then, in 1968, Larry had to cope with the loss of his beloved foster father, who died at the age of eighty-eight. It was a pretty good age for a former coal miner, but Larry and Fan were devastated to lose the man who had brought them both up as if they were his own flesh and blood, and had lost his wife so young, struggling as a widower to give them everything. Jim Hammond's death, like Ethel's, was particularly traumatic for Larry as Jim had a sudden and massive stroke while he was listening to the radio by the fire with Fan. Larry was in the other room, resting after his own illness. He heard Fan yell: "Bill! Bill! There's something wrong with your dad!". He came running and found Jim clutching at himself and groaning, unable to speak. Doctors were called, and a severe stroke was diagnosed. May's daughter Joyce, who was a qualified nurse, came round to look after Jim and sit at his bedside so that he could avoid being taken into hospital, but it was too much for an eighty-eight year old and he slipped peacefully away that night in his sleep. At least he had died at home with his family around him.

Larry later said: "I couldn't come to grips with losing someone so dear in such an unkind way." He explained their close relationship in another press interview: "To me my dad was Fan's father. He was the salt of the earth, a miner, a real gentleman. He was always very proud of me and would be waiting up when I got home from a show, however late. I had wonderful love from them all, but there's been great sorrow at their passing."

It was a disheartening and depressing time all round. So much so that Larry became ill again, more seriously this time, suffering three perforated stomach ulcers and a nervous breakdown, all as a result of the worry about his flagging career, and the heartbreak of losing his 'dad'. The doctor took one look at Larry lying in bed, white as the sheets he was lying on, and said the ulcers had haemorrhaged, like last time only worse, so he needed urgent treatment or he would die. He was rushed in a speeding ambulance to The Manor Hospital in Nuneaton where he was kept for several weeks. Heartbreakingly he once said of that desolate period, lying in his hospital bed, that he learned the very depths of depression: "At times I felt it would be easier just to go to sleep and not wake up..."

Fortunately, thanks to the kind and caring Manor Hospital nursing staff; the support of his family and friends and, importantly for Larry, the hundreds of very touching get-well cards and heartfelt messages from fans and unknown well-wishers, he pulled through and regained the will to live and to soldier on. It was a slow recovery – he even had to be taught to walk again because he had spent so long in bed. Fan said when he came home from hospital it reminded her of looking after him as a vulnerable frail little boy, back in her stepfather's house thirty years earlier. She said he just sat in a chair looking terrible, and nobody could brighten him up. Even when he was eventually able to walk again he'd barely make it to the end of Clifton Road on Fan's arm before he had to turn back, exhausted. "He was so out of breath it was frightening", Fan recalled.

Larry put the word out that he wouldn't be available for work for some time. Lying in a hospital bed had given him the opportunity to re-evaluate his life. He knew he'd been overdoing the club bookings in an attempt to forget his worries, often working seven nights a week. Fan wanted him to quit showbusiness all together before it killed him, but that was never going to happen. He couldn't walk away from the career, the life and the audience love that meant so much to him. Larry however promised himself and Fan that if he did fully recover he would never worry again. Stress about hard times, however bad, simply wasn't worth dying for.

His new carefree attitude to work paid off. A few years later, on the brink of real stardom, and about to appear at The London Palladium for the second time, Larry said: "I kept my promise about not worrying, and everything has gone right for me since then. I don't care tuppence now, which means that I can work better and I am more relaxed. Six years ago I wouldn't have even dared to walk in the back door of The Palladium, let alone go on the stage..."

Often the time when you stop desperately seeking something is the very time you find it. During this bleak period in the late sixties yet another guardian angel came to Larry's rescue...

There are certain key moments in everybody's life when something happens that changes everything. Larry was about to have one of those defining moments in 1969, and it was all thanks to a chance visit to his hospital bedside by a producer / comedy writer / agent called Peter Dulay. Peter had seen Larry work several years earlier and had been impressed. He now worked for Bob Miller Enterprises, a major showbusiness agency. He was on the look-out for new talent, and had been reminded by a colleague of this "very funny man in the Midlands". During the hospital visit, realising Larry needed a confidence and morale boost, Dulay offered to become Larry's manager, and said he would try to give him a break in London, as that is where real stars are made. At first Larry declined the offer, as he really believed he was dying, but Dulay was persistent and kept phoning to see if Larry was well enough to reconsider. Peter kept assuring Larry that he was going to make him a star. "Oh no Peter", Larry would say, "I'm too old..."

When Larry had recovered sufficiently, after the long convalescence at home with Fan, Peter Dulay was true to his word and secured him a week's booking in a high camp variety show called *A Camping We Will Go* at The Theatre Royal in London's Stratford East. The show was aimed at a predominantly gay audience, and starred drag queen 'Lana' and the *Opportunity Knocks* muscleman Tony Holland. Nursed back to his old self by Fan, and rejuvenated and re-energised by the support of his new manager, Larry got his confidence back and gave the show everything he had. It was make or break time for Larry Grayson. The week long run of *A Camping We Will Go* was a triumph for Larry, and was extended to two weeks, by popular demand. His new relaxed persona gave him a massive confidence boost on stage, which audiences adored. Larry Grayson was back on track.

The Theatre Royal in Stratford East knew they were on to a good thing and quickly transferred their new star into their next equally camp productions, *Back to Camp* and *Gaiety Box Revue*, contracting him for a longer ten week engagement. The shows were principally glitzy drag revues. In fact Larry was just about the only male performer to appear in a suit and tie, as opposed to a sequinned gown and wig, his own frock having been hung up and left behind with his previous stage name Billy Breen.

Both shows were huge successes, and Larry was described in the press as "a certain star of the future", with one reviewer saying of *Back to Camp*: "The most outstanding of this good cast is a fantastically gifted, tall and likeable comedian, new to the south of England, Larry Grayson..."

There seem to have been quite a few shows in London around that time that had a niche appeal to a gay audience. Homosexuality had recently been decriminalised in Britain, coinciding with a relaxation of the previously draconian theatre censorship laws. Suddenly there was a freedom for gay performers and gay audiences to openly get together and express and celebrate who they were. It must have been very liberating for gay people to go out and see these joyously outrageous productions without having to look over their shoulders, or disguise their enjoyment. An overtly camp performer like Larry fitted in perfectly, and was embraced by the enthusiastic audiences. In time the more militant members of the gay community would turn on Larry and be positively vitriolic with their criticism of his stereotypically camp style, but that was still quite a few years in the future. For now he was welcomed, feted and adored by the London gay fraternity.

Things started to snowball more and more rapidly for Larry from that point on. Famed Soho impresario Paul Raymond came along to see *Gaiety Box Revue*, and was so blown away by Larry that he signed him up on the spot to be the host and compere of his forthcoming new adult revue, *Birds of a Feather*. The show was due to open a few months later at The Royalty Theatre, in the heart of London's theatreland, hot on the heels of the runaway success of Raymond's sex farce *Pyjama Tops*, featuring unashamed nudity in the curvaceous form of soft porn star Fiona Richmond.

Birds of a Feather was another all-male drag revue but, being backed by wealthy entrepreneur and porn baron Paul Raymond, it was on a much bigger and more lavish high profile scale in a major London theatre. Larry Grayson was now a West End Star. Again Larry resisted the temptation to return to female impersonations, and appeared in suit and tie, in amongst all the other glamorously-attired drag artistes.

Paul Raymond invested a huge amount of money in *Birds of a Feather*, which boasted in its theatre programme: "The world's greatest female impersonators". Raymond insisted on the most extravagantly glamorous costumes and sets, but his massive investment in style over content didn't pay off unfortunately. *The Times* theatre critic said the show was: "as flashily characterless as candy floss". Ouch! The only redeeming feature of the entire show, according to the reviewers, was the hilarious host and compere, Larry Grayson. Even Paul Raymond himself later said the only good thing to come out of *Birds of a Feather* was his long association and enduring friendship with Larry. It seems those kind of gay appeal shows, hugely successful in smaller fringe venues, were not yet capable of attracting large enough audiences to sustain a West End run. Suffering considerable financial losses, due to the empty seats, Paul Raymond was forced to close the hugely expensive show after just seventeen days.

However "England's Comedy Sensation", as Larry Grayson was billed by Paul Raymond, kept going from strength to strength...

9

... the big time beckons... at last...

1970, notwithstanding the *Birds of a Feather* disaster in the early part of the year, was the year that changed everything for Larry Grayson. Despite the more prestigious venues Larry had been playing, it was at a slightly seedy Soho nightclub, an old haunt of The Kray Twins in fact, where his big break came, at long last. Al Burnett, the owner of the West End's Stork Club, a notorious prostitute pick-up joint, gave Larry a two week engagement in The Stork Room. Larry went down so well on the opening night that Burnett immediately extended the booking to twelve weeks.

Peter Dulay, disappointed by the abrupt termination of the *Birds of a Feather* contract, needed somebody who could open doors that he simply couldn't, so he called upon his friends and contacts to help him salvage something positive for his new client. Peter was the son of comedy magician Benson Dulay, so he knew a lot of people in the business. The most influential of his contacts was Michael Grade, who had become a friend while he was writing for Michael's client Leslie Crowther. Dulay phoned talent-spotting agent Michael Grade and said he'd found a new comedy sensation he was now managing, and he invited Grade to come along to see his new protégé during the Stork Club engagement. At the time Michael was working for his father, Leslie Grade, one of the top theatrical and variety agents in the country, who only looked after the biggest and the best stars, most notably at that time Norman Wisdom, Morecambe & Wise and Bruce Forsyth.

Michael, now Lord Grade, told me that the whisky and soda he was given to drink when he arrived at the rather sleazy Stork Club was served in a teacup and saucer, in case the police came in, because they weren't officially licensed for selling liquor. Michael Grade had given up a perfectly good Sunday evening and had driven all the way into central London, he was sipping whisky from a teacup, and then his heart sank as he realised the unimaginatively named *The Ha Ha Revue* he was about to watch in The Stork Room was little more than a transvestite drag-fest. Despite his faith in Peter Dulay's judgment he said he began to wonder what on earth he was doing there. Larry however was one of the few members of the cast that night who was wearing smart male attire, doing the gossipy stand-up act leaning on the chair, the act we were all soon to know and love. Larry only filled in for four or five minutes while the drag acts got changed, but that was all it took. Grade was blown away. He knew a potential star when he saw one. He went to the communal dressing room with Peter Dulay after the show, which Michael says was a bizarre experience with all the drag acts getting changed all around them, but he took to Larry right away and signed him up to the illustrious Grade Organisation the very next morning.

Of course this meant that Larry was paying management fees to Peter Dulay, and also agent fees to The Grade Organisation. It was a lot of commission being taken from his earnings, but then they were getting him prestigious and lucrative bookings that he thought were never going to come.

Michael Grade realised that his first task, if Larry was to become a major mainstream star, was to extricate him from the drag shows, the gay revues, and the seedy late night dives, and put him back in a more conventional entertainment environment. The Grade family controlled a lot of British entertainment in those days, so he had a word with one of his influential uncles, theatre impresario Bernard Delfont, and secured his new client a summer season in a top show in one of Britain's most vibrant seaside resorts. It was the 1970 summer season at The Theatre Royal in Brighton – a show called *Startime*, with top radio and TV comedian Arthur Askey and pop singer Kathy Kirby sharing star billing.

This was a classy show with quality acts aimed at a family audience. Larry's recent performances, working for people like Paul Raymond and Al Burnett, had been a little more adult in nature. Grade knew that Larry's sometimes risqué club material had to be vetted and gone through with a fine tooth comb for Brighton's *Startime*, or Uncle Bernard Delfont would have vetoed the booking. If that happened his rather prudish father, Leslie Grade, Delfont's brother, might possibly question the signing of Michael's new discovery. Larry's material was worked on and perfected, and consequently his spots in *Startime* were very well received. In fact a local newspaper review of their opening night praised the show for being suitable for all the family, despite a couple of saucy seaside postcard type jokes, and singled Larry's performance out as "so side-splittingly hilarious that the audience yelled for more and gave him a tremendous ovation". Michael Grade's instincts had been correct.

Special guest on that show was Hetty King, one of the last survivors of the days of 'old time music hall'. At the unbelievable age of eighty-seven she was still doing her act as a male impersonator. The irony can't have been lost on former female impersonator Larry. Even though he was forty-seven by then, Larry was a fresh-faced youngster next to Hetty King and seventy-year-old Askey.

Larry Grayson took Brighton by storm – so much so that his long-running summer season engagement was quickly followed by a pantomime booking, also at The Theatre Royal in Brighton: *Goldilocks and the Three Bears*, starring Dora Bryan and Valentine Dyall (aka BBC radio's 'The Man in Black'). The story goes that Dora Bryan, who lived in the Brighton area, had gone along to see the *Startime* summer show and laughed until she cried at Larry's spot. After the show she contacted the theatre management and said: "Can I have that lovely man in my pantomime?" They wrote an additional character (the circus ringmaster) into the script especially for him, but the writers struggled to capture Larry's unique style. In the end they gave up and gave him free reign. Dora Bryan said it didn't really matter what went in the script as, when the two of them were on stage together, they never said the same thing two nights running. She loved Larry and worked with him when ever she could after that, enjoying his company off-stage and finding his unique on-stage style hilarious. Larry became close friends with Dora and her cricketer husband Bill Lawton, and was like an uncle to her three children.

Before the pantomime with Dora Bryan though Michael Grade had some very exciting news for Larry. He had managed to get him a short first-half spot on a spectacular variety bill at the legendary London Palladium. The show was to run for two whole weeks in the lead up to the panto season. The big name stars of the show were character comedian Dick Emery, pianist Russ Conway, singer and siffleur (whistler) Roger Whittaker, and squeaky clean sixties pop group Herman's Hermits, all introduced by compere Pete

Murray, the Radio 2 DJ. Larry was near the bottom of the bill, and only on stage for nine minutes, but Larry Grayson was at last playing the number one variety theatre in the country, the venue every up and coming comedian dreamed of playing.

He was thrilled to be appearing there, feeling that at long last he had arrived. He said those two weeks were the highlight of his career at that time. All the hard work and heartache had finally paid off. This was the big time. In his Palladium dressing room on the first night Larry sat there thinking about the little schoolboy in Nuneaton who was mocked for saying he was going to be a star when he couldn't even sing, dance or play a musical instrument. It must have been a very gratifying moment. The only small shadow over this otherwise momentous experience was the thought that he would have liked his foster parents and his real mum to have been there to witness it and share it with him. They'd seen the years of struggle and toil, it was such a shame they never saw their boy reap the rewards.

Meanwhile, on the opening night inside The Palladium auditorium, Michael Grade was sitting there in the front stalls with his business partner Billy Marsh, and his father Leslie Grade, who were both seeing Michael's new signing for the first time. The press were all in as well, so it was an anxious time. Would Larry hold his nerve under the pressure of appearing at the most famous theatre in Britain? Would a sophisticated Palladium audience get his humour? The problem with Larry's act was that there were no jokes. A well-known visiting American comedian once saw Larry's act written down on paper in his dressing room and asked him incredulously: "Do you really get laughs with this stuff?!" You either got it or you didn't, but Larry's personality drew you into his quirky world and carried you along once you were on his wavelength. Michael Grade told me that his fondest memory of his time with Larry was that first huge laugh at The Palladium. The audience got Larry straight away and roared with approval. Michael breathed a huge sigh of relief, having wondered if Billy Marsh and his father might just witness his new signing walking off to the sound of his own feet.

Larry's contribution to the Palladium show was show-stealing, and the Grade family found themselves looking after another future star of stage and screen. The major London theatre critics, who were seeing Larry for the first time, loved this 'newcomer', although *The Times* published a somewhat back-handed compliment: "For me the evening's most cheering item was the Palladium debut of an attenuated limp-wristed comic named Larry Grayson".

The Daily Express were more fulsome with their praise: "A talented original comedian". One somewhat pompous reviewer said of Larry: "His quips, with many asides, fell on fertile soil, garnering some of the heartiest laughter heard at The Palladium in many moons". However *The Daily Telegraph* hit the nail on the head much more succinctly: "He is funny".

At the time Larry told one journalist, commenting about his thirty-three-year showbiz apprenticeship: "It's all happening and I can hardly believe it. After all these years, it's like a dream come true."

Strangely Larry didn't get seduced by the glamorous life in the showbiz capital. Throughout the first week of the run at The Palladium, he commuted home to Nuneaton and Fan every night by train, arriving at their Clifton Road house around midnight, then setting off back to London in time for the first house the following day. Reluctantly he had to stay away from home during the second week, because he had pantomime rehearsals during the day. He never really did like staying in London, even at the height of his fame, during *The Generation Game*.

After the success of The Palladium run The Grade Organisation were subsequently able to book Larry Grayson for more prestigious and increasingly high profile appearances. The following year there was another summer season, supporting family favourite comedian Leslie Crowther at The Festival Hall in Paignton for fourteen weeks. The show was called *Crowther's in Town* and also featured famed "Desert Song" tenor John Hanson and Basil Brush. Incidentally Basil was billed as "Britain's funniest fox". I'm not sure how many other funny foxes we had at the time, but Basil certainly deserved the title. Larry was still near the bottom of the bill, but at least he was being noticed in bigger productions in better venues. Success breeds success and appearing in these top well-attended shows gave Larry even more self-confidence which he exuded on stage, making his already memorable performances better than ever. Michael Grade told me it was not only a good show and a successful show, but it was also a very happy show. The cast all got on well as friends, and respected one another as professionals. In fact John Hanson became a lifelong friend of Larry and Leslie Crowther described Larry Grayson as: "One of the funniest comedians I have had the pleasure of working with. Everyone loves him."

Larry thoroughly enjoyed his time in Paignton, making lots of new friends. One of the young follow-spot operators in The Festival Hall, Kevin Bishop, later a top executive at the BBC, recalls befriending Larry and having great fun with him that summer. Kevin was a local lad and, having taken pity on Larry waiting at the bus stop after one of the first shows, he drove him to and from the theatre every day for the rest of the season. Kevin recalls what a fun and happy summer that was. He also remembers how much he laughed every night at Larry's spot in the show. Although Larry was well disciplined and totally professional, sticking to a similar structure with his material and always keeping rigidly to his allotted time, nevertheless the spot was never the same twice and there was always something new to amuse the crew.

Sunday nights were the highlight of the week socially because it was the only night when there were no shows to perform. Sid James, the legendary comic actor, was appearing just down the road in *The Mating Season* at The Pavilion Theatre in Torquay, and he used to throw big parties, to which they were all invited. Sid was famous for living life to the full, so these were wild nights. Comedians are traditionally careful with money, so Larry didn't splash out on parties himself, but Kevin says he was extremely popular because he was so funny and such fun to be around.

Whilst in Paignton with *Crowther's in Town*, in the summer of 1971, Larry indulged his belief and interest in fortune-telling once again. He went along with some of the company to see a local end-of-the-pier crystal-ball-gazing clairvoyant called Madame Credo, in nearby Brixham. Much to his somewhat sceptical amusement she predicted that he would soon be propelled from near the bottom of the bill to the top of the bill, and inside a year she foretold that he would be making regular appearances on television. Madame Credo also said a 'big building' would be a major part of his rapid rise to stardom. Larry later interpreted that somewhat vague prediction as his imminent return to The London Palladium. Personally I think it unlikely that seaside fortune-tellers really have the gift of seeing into the future, but she had no doubt seen his summer show and could obviously spot a future star when she saw one. She'd probably also read his rave reviews in the local press. Despite his unswerving belief in fortune tellers and clairvoyants, Larry didn't dare take too much notice of this thrilling vision of his future, but Madame Credo turned out to be absolutely right. Just a couple of years later Larry said: "At that time there didn't seem to be even the remotest chance of (Madame Credo's predictions) coming true, but here I am on TV..."

Madame Credo's real name was Helen Edden, and Larry kept in touch with her for many years, often consulting with her when there were important decisions to be made, including whether or not he should accept the job as the new host of *The Generation Game*. She even appeared as a guest on one of his ATV shows.

After Paignton it was a thrilling return to The London Palladium for Larry in *The Val Doonican Show*, November 1971. Star comedy impressionist Mike Yarwood was supposed to be sharing top billing in the show, but he pulled out at the eleventh hour, "indisposed". The hugely popular Yarwood was hastily replaced by last minute booking Norman Vaughan, whose comedy career was on the wane by that point. This probably did Larry a favour as it allowed him to win over the hearts and the laughter of the audience. He still wasn't topping the bill, but it was a major step up the showbusiness ladder, supporting such a major star as Doonican in Britain's most prestigious variety venue.

Whilst still in Paignton the ambitious follow-spot operator Kevin Bishop offered to go with Larry to London to act as his road manager for the forthcoming run at The Palladium. Kevin says Larry couldn't afford to pay him, but he did get all his expenses paid. Whilst he was helping Larry out at The Palladium Kevin became friendly with Larry's manager, Peter Dulay, who had just bought the television rights to *Candid Camera*, and was about to re-launch it back on to British screens. Dulay was impressed by Bishop and gave him his first job in TV, the start of another highly successful career.

Larry received yet more rave reviews in the press for his second appearance at The Palladium, stealing the limelight from many of the other top acts on the bill. John Barber, theatre critic for *The Daily Telegraph* gave another back-handed compliment, saying Larry was "like a quick-fire, back-street, off-colour Oscar Wilde". He sweetened his comment though by saying: "Larry Grayson proves again to be the brightest of comedians. I find him very funny." The London *Evening News*, the *Daily Express* and *The Stage* critics were equally enthusiastic, and all made favourable comparisons with established comedian Frankie Howerd... something which didn't please Frankie Howerd unfortunately. Howerd, an insecure performer at the best of times, decided he was the victim of plagiarism, and took an instant dislike to Larry. In fact their acts were very different, but you could see why critics saw a vague similarity in their high camp gossipy performance styles. Truthfully it was just a case of lazy journalism on the part of the critics, but Frankie Howerd went through life saying that Larry had pinched his act.

Another boost to Larry's rapidly increasing bankability in London, and his imminent meteoric rise to fame, came from a close friend and like-minded showbusiness contemporary. Nationally-renowned female impersonator Danny La Rue had his own eponymous nightclub in ritzy Mayfair, where he performed extravagant and glamorously camp comedy revues nightly. It was the fashionable place to be seen, and Ronnie Corbett had been discovered there by David Frost and turned into a television star through *The Frost Report*. Of course a club called Danny La Rue's couldn't operate without Danny La Rue as the star of the show, so he had found himself working seven nights a week, year in, year out, ever since the club opened eight years previously. However much you love performing body and soul can only take so much. Danny couldn't keep up that punishing workload for ever. One day, in late 1971, Jack Hanson, Danny's manager and long-time life partner, came home to find Danny curled up on the floor in the foetal position, unable to get up, and on the verge of a nervous breakdown. Doctors insisted he take a complete rest from any sort of work for two weeks. But what about the nightclub? There was only one friend and fellow performer Danny trusted to fill his high-heeled diamante shoes, so the first phone call he asked Jack to make was to Larry Grayson. Danny showed Larry the revue and asked him if he could link it all together in his place, and do with it what ever he pleased. Larry asked how long he could have for a solo spot to close the show, and was told no more than twenty minutes. That was more than enough.

A big splash was made in the press about Danny taking his first holiday for eight years, with of course no mention of the nervous breakdown. Danny was photographed handing over the keys to his nightclub to Larry Grayson, "direct from his great London Palladium triumph..." Danny La Rue told the press: "Larry is the funniest man I have seen in a decade". He privately told Larry if he had turned down the offer of taking over the club he would have closed the place down for two weeks, as there was nobody else he held in such high esteem. Danny, who had a total aversion to flying, went off by road for his much-needed two week spell of rest and recuperation in Portugal's sunny seaside resort of Estoril with Jack Hanson, leaving Larry Grayson holding the fort at Danny La Rue's in Mayfair.

Larry used this golden opportunity to showcase his talent to the movers and shakers of the television and theatre industries who frequented the club, and he stormed the place every night, getting ever more glowing reviews in the press. His success at The Palladium, followed so closely by this high profile headlining at Danny's club was a major breakthrough for

Larry as he had never been able to conquer London before, and London was undoubtedly the showbusiness capital, as Peter Dulay had prophetically said: where real stars are made.

One London theatre critic said, after seeing Larry at Danny La Rue's: "He is undoubtedly the IN comic of the year, and if causing non-stop laughter from his very entrance is any criterion, then Larry Grayson is a star already."

Larry's triumphant two weeks performing for the glitterati at Danny La Rue's went so well that Larry became hailed in fashionable London showbiz circles as the new Sid Field, a highly-revered post-war camp comedian, also from the Midlands, who sadly died too young for most of us to remember him. The comparison was a real accolade however because comedy legends like Eric Morecambe and Tony Hancock spoke in hushed tones of Sid Field's genius, and cited him as an inspiration and a major influence on their work.

Kevin Bishop, who was Larry's unpaid road manager during the two weeks at The Palladium and the two weeks at Danny's club, still says those were the best four weeks of his life. He says it was so exciting because everybody who was anybody seemed to want to meet the 'new' comedy discovery. Even Liberace came to see Larry in his dressing-room one night after a show at Danny's club.

10

... the power of television creates a star...

Michael Grade knew the importance of television in that seminal decade, now often referred to as The Golden Age of TV, so he rang some of the many television producers he knew, securing Larry a couple of minor guest appearances on ITV shows like *David Nixon's Magic Box*, and *The Leslie Crowther Show*. Fan said she just sat and cried the first time she saw him on television. "My Billy!" she sobbed, "That's my Billy!".

William G Stewart, who produced *The Leslie Crowther Show*, had never seen Larry work, and asked him to run through what he was going to do on the show so that they could rehearse the camera shots. Larry, who wasn't used to the strict discipline of television, looked horrified and said: "I don't rehearse – I just make it up as I go along!". William insisted on Larry at least talking him through roughly what he was going to do. On the night of course he did something completely different, but he went down well nonetheless. After the show William congratulated Larry on a great performance, then naively asked what all this 'gay day' business was all about. Larry told him: "If you don't know then you aren't one of us."

At least ITV wasn't flooded with complaints like the BBC had been fifteen years earlier. Times were changing and society, even the blue-rinsed outraged middle class, was becoming more liberal-minded. It was useful experience and a promising start to Larry's television career, but truthfully nothing earth-shattering happened immediately and nobody took much notice. A year later though the show would come along that was to turn

Larry Grayson into a household name, a much beloved entertainer, and an overnight star, thirty-five years in the making.

ATV, the major Midlands supplier to the ITV network at the time, was run by Michael Grade's other impresario uncle, Lew Grade. In those golden days of television cash-rich ATV had massive programme budgets and could therefore afford to be the purveyors of lavish and spectacular variety entertainment on television. In the early part of 1972 they were about to launch a major new network series called *Saturday Variety*. Michael Grade phoned ATV's entertainment booker Alec Fyne and asked him to take a look at Larry. Fyne liked what he saw and offered Larry a spot on one show. Michael Grade held his nerve and said that his client was worth more than just one appearance. Fyne eventually caved in and said Larry could appear on the first three shows, including a four minute guest spot on the very first programme in the series, with Dorothy Squires topping the bill in her first major television appearance in ten years.

The Grade family connection possibly made Alec look seriously at this 'newcomer', but it was Larry's warm and hilarious appeal which earned him guaranteed appearances on such a big new show. Alec Fyne was taking a risk in a way and could have booked any number of more established comedians who would have been happy to do the shows. His faith was well placed however – Larry Grayson was an instant success. ITV was inundated, not with complaints this time, but enthusiastic plaudits asking why Larry had not been on television before and begging to see more of this hilarious 'new' comedian. Mighty oaks from tiny acorns grow, as they say. Uncle Lew was impressed too by his nephew's discovery and immediately got Alec Fyne to invite Larry back for yet more shows, after the first three. The reaction was every bit as enthusiastic, so Larry became a regular on the series and ended up appearing in sixteen of the twenty-six *Saturday Variety* shows which were seen that year on ITV.

Saturday Variety was transmitted live from the ATV studios in Elstree. Larry travelled down by train and walked up to the gatehouse with his suitcase in hand. The security guard, after a couple of weeks, prophetically said: "It won't be long before you're driving in here in your own Rolls Royce..."

Once again Kevin Bishop was enlisted to help out as Larry's road manager for his appearances on *Saturday Variety*. I get the impression Larry always needed somebody with him when he was doing a big show – a friend to reassure him and tell him that he was doing okay, and remind him how funny he was. Even on stage he couldn't be alone – the ever-present bentwood chair was some comfort and support for an inherently insecure performer.

Larry needed to be liked. He once told a journalist during a press conference for a big show: "It is tremendously important to me that I am liked. If there is someone in a room who doesn't like me, I can sense it immediately. It worries me. I have to do something about it." He needn't have worried, as everybody seemed to like Larry, but it illustrates his ingrained insecurity.

Keeping him grounded as always, Fan greeted Larry's exciting news about his forthcoming first appearance on ITV's *Saturday Variety*, with a hesitant frown and the words: "You know we never watch ITV... and we're not going to miss *Dixon of Dock Green*..."

Larry Grayson's first ever words on that game-changing debut on *Saturday Variety* were: "Well I'm worn out before I start!". Those words could have almost been referring to the thirty-five year struggle it had taken to get there, but instead they set the tone for an almost inexplicably hilarious act. Suddenly television audiences couldn't get enough of this lovable, but self-pitying hypochondriac gossip.

The catchphrases and the regular bits of business arrived on-screen fully formed, having been tried and tested for years on club and theatre audiences, so they caught on immediately. The bentwood chair acted as a security blanket for Larry as a nervy performer, but it quickly became his distinctively unique trademark. In a camp fashion he'd lean on the chair back, as if for support, then he'd run his finger along the top of it and look at the digit with mock disgust saying: "Look at the muck on 'ere!" For punctuation half way through his spot he'd say: "Let's have a change of scenery..." then simply move his chair from one side of him to the other.

The catchphrases were also a major part of his instant TV success: "What a gay day!" ... "She's as common as dirt!" ... "Seems like a nice boy!" ... and of course: "Shut that door!" His outrageous cast of unseen friends were all there too, vividly painted in hilarious word pictures, having been in Larry's head for years: Everard, Slack Alice, Apricot Lil, etc. It was a rare thing – an experienced and highly assured middle-aged performer with a finely tuned well-rehearsed act that most of the viewing public had never seen before. He was so unusual and so accomplished television viewers must have thought he'd been flown in from another planet.

Larry enjoyed the instant stardom, but never complained that it had taken so long to arrive, and had come so late in life. He said at the time, of his long showbiz apprenticeship: "People say what a pity it didn't happen before, but I am glad it didn't. I wouldn't have missed it for anything."

A major part of Larry's act on TV seemed to revolve around his various aches, pains and illnesses. A lot of them were real. He once went on stage with his shoulder hurting so badly he could hardly move his head. He picked up his famous chair and moaned "Oh, the agony!", only to find the audience fell about in hysterics. Having found that his discomfort was a source of great amusement he built it into his act. He would complain that he'd woken up as limp as a vicar's handshake, then regale the audience with his various ailments: "I had it all down this side yesterday, I've got it all down this side today... I can't wait for tomorrow!" When the roar of approval had died down he would get a second belly laugh by adding, pointing limp-wristedly into the audience: "You suffer from it as well, don't you? ... I can tell from the way you're sitting..." Larry would then say that he had to use special ointment to ease the pain: "I normally use 'Fiery Jack'... but I seem to have lost his address..."

As a result of this hilarious hypochondria the great British television viewing public, as is their wont, sent Larry bottles of liniment and patent pain relievers by the crate. He made an appeal at the time: "Stop it, please. No more liniment. I have enough to fill a couple of baths. Viewers keep sending in bottles of liniment and all their fancy cures, but my back's a lot better..." Then with his usual subversive impish humour he added with a toss of his head: "Trouble is my foot's playing up now..."

It was Larry's time. He'd waited long enough for it. Camp humour was not only more acceptable in the early 1970s, it was positively fashionable. *Are You Being Served* first came on air in the same year, with newcomer John Inman camping it up with his famous cries of "I'm free!"; one of Dick Emery's most popular characters was the camp floppy-hat-wearing Clarence, aka 'Honky Tonks'; Kenny Everett's high camp could be heard on radio, and later seen on TV; plus of course perennial favourites like Kenneth Williams and Frankie Howerd were getting ever more outrageous, and the public were lapping it up.

After all the years and years of trying to claw his way up to the top, when it eventually happened the fame and success escalated very rapidly. Within weeks of his triumphant residency on *Saturday Variety* Larry was invited to appear in a special Royal Gala Show in aid of The British Olympics Appeal Fund, which was to be staged at The London Palladium on May 22nd

1972. It was an international all-star bill, including The Osmonds, Michael Caine, Lily Tomlin, Roger Moore and Des O'Connor, hosted by top American comedy double act Rowan & Martin. Larry was thrilled by this great honour, especially as it meant meeting The Queen and Prince Philip after the show. Larry had always been a great Royalist, so much so that he would always stand up when ever the national anthem was played, and he even stood up to listen to The Queen's Speech after lunch every Christmas Day.

Fan said it was one of his finest moments, shaking hands with the Royal couple in the line-up after the show. She'd worried that he'd be nervous, but he took it all in his stride. The Queen asked him if he'd enjoyed himself, and wondered if he'd been nervous, adding: "They tell me that when you are on a variety show early on it is very difficult". Larry made her laugh by saying: "I'm used to it. I've always been on early Ma'am...". Making The Queen laugh was a very proud achievement for Larry, and he treasured the photograph of that moment.

An equally big thrill was working with the top of the bill that night – Liza Minnelli. Liza was of course Judy Garland's daughter. In 1964 Larry had treated himself to a front stalls seat to see the legendary mother and daughter team perform live together on stage at The London Palladium, which he said was a truly special and most magical night. He said though that he never thought in his wildest dreams that nearly ten years later he would be on the same stage with his all-time idol's daughter, in front of Her Majesty The Queen. It really was a dream come true.

The offers kept flooding in for 'new star' Larry Grayson, which was understandably thrilling for him after all these years, but the determination not to succumb to another breakdown made him cautious not to overdo things, and to take his newfound success at a steady pace. This turned out to be a very shrewd ploy, as it made him much more selective about what he did agree to do, and it made the offers more attractive and bigger in scale. He was now being invited to top the bill in prestigious venues for pantomimes and summer seasons but, more importantly, ATV were so keen on their new protégé that they offered him his own six-part television series entitled, not too surprisingly, *Shut That Door*.

Larry had always been able to create all his own material for his theatre and club work. It really just sort of evolved over the years, as he developed his persona and style of performing, changing bits here and bits there, but basically doing the same stuff week after week. Television however, as all comedians have found when they first appear on the small screen, gobbles up material at an alarming rate, so for the first time Larry had to work with scriptwriters. His manager Peter Dulay was a comedy writer himself, so he had nominated himself to keep a watchful eye over the television scripts, which Larry pretty much ignored anyway, preferring to go out there and 'wing it'. Most writers seemed to find it difficult to tap into Larry's very peculiar way of being funny. Even legendary comedy writer Barry Cryer told me that he was once commissioned to write scripts for Larry in those early days, but none of the material was right and Barry asked for his credit to be removed from the show, as none of his scripts ended up being used.

Larry once commented that his greatest scriptwriters were his two sisters, adding: "They'd be the funniest act ever!". His style of humour just came from the Nuneaton women he knew, and the rhythms of their speech, especially when they gossiped.

Larry didn't really do jokes or gags, which proved bewildering to writers who were used to working for quickfire gagsmiths like Jimmy Tarbuck and Bob Monkhouse. Not only that but Larry was frustrating to write for because he wasn't very good at learning lines, so scripts were anathema to him. In his early days of doing television Larry befriended a musician called Bernie Sharp who seemed to have the exact same sense of humour as Larry, and was on the same wavelength. This was just what Larry needed. They would sit in the dressing room together gossiping about Slack Alice and Everard's antics, and all of Larry's ailments, making each other laugh. Not much was written down – maybe the odd note on the back of an envelope or a fag packet – but Larry would absorb the best bits and then regurgitate them in front of the cameras, to the delight of the studio audience. It was a system that worked a treat and Bernie Sharp was Larry's main 'writer' all through his television career. The other constant who enhanced most of Larry's television shows was long-suffering musician Dennis Plowright, who was his bespectacled accompanist, pianist and the mute butt of many of Larry's hilariously barbed comments.

1972 was an incredible year for Larry Grayson – *Saturday Variety*, the Royal Gala Show, and his own television series. The accolades just kept coming. He played cabaret at The Savoy Hotel, and then later that same year, the famous British showbusiness organisation The Grand Order of The Water Rats presented Larry with their much-coveted 'Personality of the Year' award, an honour which had been given to none less than Morecambe

& Wise the previous year. This was the long-awaited recognition for the little fostered lad from Nuneaton who couldn't sing, dance or play a musical instrument. At last, just like he'd always said he would be, he really was a star.

Larry's astonishing year had one last crowning glory. He was given his own Christmas Special on ITV, which was exciting enough, but, just as he was taking his emotional final bows during the recording of that Christmas show, an unexpected guest walked on to the studio floor. It was Eamonn Andrews with his famous red book. He approached a disbelieving and suddenly even more emotional Larry with the immortal words: "Larry Grayson – This Is Your Life!"

Larry had been told to expect an after-show party, but this was beyond his wildest dreams. He was taken backstage to recover his composure and relax for a few minutes while they transformed the ATV studio in Elstree for this special festive edition of *This Is Your Life*, which was transmitted on December 27th 1972 as a major part of ITV's Christmas schedule.

Larry was like a kid in a sweet shop as all his friends and family came on to pay tribute to this dear sweet man who made everybody laugh so much. The seat of honour, next to Larry, was given to Fan of course. Poor Fan was not used to being in the spotlight herself, and looked somewhat bewildered, though delighted for her foster brother. Of course Larry had no idea who was waiting behind the scenes to spring the next surprise. Famous friends like Dora Bryan, John Hanson, Leslie Crowther, Danny La Rue, Mike & Bernie Winters, and Lionel Blair were all there. Equally heartwarming and thrilling for Larry though were the non-celebrities who had been invited to come along. His older foster sister May and her husband Charlie took their place next to Fan. May's daughter Joyce and her husband Reg were there as well. Larry was then delighted to be reunited with 'Uncle' Alf and 'Aunty' Nell Freeman who had given him his first break with The Vary Lites when he was just fourteen years old. The production team had even managed to track down Ellen Taylor and Carol Cox, two of the nurses who had primarily been responsible for nursing him back to health, just before his big break came.

The final surprise came when Eamonn introduced a remarkably spry eighty-year-old Harry Leslie who talked about his memories of Billy Breen and *Tomorrow's Stars*. But the last word quite rightly went to Fan. Eamonn Andrews turned to her and asked: "Fan – you are the most important person in Larry's life, and you've seen him up, and you've seen him down. Did you really believe he was going to make it?" She simply answered, with all sincerity: "Yes I did". With that Eamonn presented a teary-eyed Larry Grayson with his much-treasured big red book and said: "Happy New Year Larry – This Is Your Life"...

When it was all over, and she'd had the last word, Fan broke down in tears. She explained afterwards: "My Larry, that frail little child I'd devoted my life to, was a star! I just couldn't stop the tears from rolling down my cheeks. But as the audience clapped and shouted I knew all those years of struggle had not been in vain."

They all then went into the Green Room for a joyous party, ending what Larry said was one of the greatest days of his life, at the end of the greatest year of his life. What a pity Ethel, Jim and Alice weren't there to share it with him...

11

... enjoying success... and a phantom romance...

Larry Grayson once said that at the beginning of 1972, his turning point year, he went from earning an average of £75 a week at the beginning of the year to £6,000 a week by the end. That would still be very good money now, but back then it was an astronomical figure.

He suddenly found himself in the money for the first time in his life, however Larry didn't let it go to his head, and he refused to leave his beloved Nuneaton. He didn't even want to move from his long time home with Fan in Clifton Road, but his manager Peter Dulay insisted that a big star couldn't possibly live in a terraced house, so Larry somewhat reluctantly agreed to a move, with Fan and 'Peter the poodle', to a bigger detached house on Hinckley Road, a nicer area which was still on the outskirts of Nuneaton. He called the new house 'The Garlands', as a tribute to his idol Judy Garland. As he said about staying in his home town: "I like it there. It keeps me on the level. They won't let me get big-headed." Of the new house he said: "It's not a mansion, there's no swimming pool. It's just home for me and Fan." It was almost as though he was embarrassed by his newfound wealth. The one concession to grandeur was a flagpole in the garden, to which a flag was attached and hoisted as a landmark when visitors were expected.

Also in the space of that defining year of 1972 Larry had gone from a situation where nobody outside of Nuneaton knew who he was, to a point where he couldn't go anywhere without being mobbed by adoring fans. Michael Grade once said to Larry's manager Peter Dulay, as they fought off crowds of cheering fans, in order to get Larry into his car after a show: "We've created a monster!".

The moment that consolidated Larry's fame for him, and made him feel like the local lad made good, came in 1973 when he was first booked to appear at The Coventry Theatre, previously known as The Coventry Hippodrome. Sadly it was demolished in 2002, but in its heyday it boasted a massive auditorium, seating over two thousand people. In all the years he'd worked the clubs in that area he had never been a big enough name to appear in that magnificent venue where he had seen so many spectacular musicals and top variety shows as a child with the Hammonds, and later with his friend Tom Proctor.

Larry said during the rehearsals for the show: "I used to walk by this theatre when I was a boy and say to myself, 'I would give anything to play there'... At the time I couldn't even afford to buy a seat and see the shows." He added: "I still really can't believe it. When I step out on that stage tomorrow night it is going to be a terrifying experience, and quite a responsibility. I feel I shall know them all – like personal friends."

It was a disappointment to Larry that even his first proper manager Evie Taylor had never managed to book him into the one theatre that held so many magical memories for him. It was a piece of poetic serendipity therefore that he should appear there for the first time, topping the bill, starring in his own fiftieth birthday show. Supporting him were Rod Hull & Emu, The Kaye Sisters, piano duo Rostal & Schaefer, and a young talented impressionist called Dave Evans (father of international comedy star Lee Evans).

All Larry's old friends who were still working the local club circuit came along to pat him on the back and congratulate him on his newfound and hard-earned fame. In his own words he felt like the star who had come home. One of his old female friends, who was still working the club circuit, told Larry, with undisguised relief: "Ooh Lal! Fame hasn't spoilt you. You haven't changed!" He said: "Of course I haven't changed! I haven't grown another head! Pop round tomorrow for a cup o' tea..."

The show received rave reviews in the press, citing Larry as one of a rare breed of entertainer, a real individual comic talent and a true star, at the peak of his powers as a comedian. The show's director, Dick Hurran, was quoted as saying: "I've worked with nearly all the big stars, but I've never worked with such a gentleman."

One night during that triumphant run Mrs Proctor came along, the mother of Larry's dead friend Tom. Larry was thrilled to see her and asked her what she thought Tom would have made of his stardom and all the trappings of fame. It was an emotional moment when she reassured Larry that Tom would have been delighted for his friend.

One thing many stars say when they first become famous is that they can no longer walk down the street. The good thing for Larry about staying in Nuneaton was that everybody already knew him, and nothing much changed. The townsfolk were all pleased for their local lad made good, and might say "Saw you on the telly last night", but he was still greeted as he always had been: "Morning Bill!" ... "Alright Bill?" ... "How're you doing m'duck?" ... "How's Fan?". He was treated just the same, not like a freak, which suited him perfectly.

Larry genuinely liked people, so long as they treated him with the respect and courtesy that he showed them. He loved his fans, and he was a prolific letter writer. He had a little portable typewriter which he took nearly everywhere with him, bashing away with two fingers at great speed to keep his friends and fans updated with his life. Private letters to close friends could be whimsical, quite risqué, packed with salacious gossip, and often hilarious. Equally his letters could be wistful, or even downright melancholic, depending upon his mood. If he was away from home and didn't have the typewriter handy he would write in longhand on hotel notepaper or what ever writing material he could scrounge. For years Larry prided himself in writing back personally to every single fan letter he received, and enclosing an autographed photograph. During the height of his fame, when fan letters were arriving by the sack full, this became physically impossible, so he had to reluctantly enlist help.

He regarded his dedicated fans as true friends and would sometimes enter into lengthy correspondence with them. One such fan was a lady called Pauline Pearson. Pauline had attended one of Larry's stage shows in the early 1970s, at the start of his years of fame, and had tentatively, and almost apologetically, written Larry a short letter saying how much she'd enjoyed the show, and telling him what a big fan she was of his television series. Larry, to her delight, sent her a genuinely heartfelt and grateful personal response on his own headed notepaper. That was the start of a very endearing and lengthy correspondence which went on for over twenty years, right up to Larry's death. As well as letters packed with news and gossip they exchanged birthday cards and Christmas cards every year. Pauline kept all Larry's sometimes quite lengthy letters, and when she passed away many years later her son donated the carefully preserved collection to The Nuneaton Museum & Art Gallery. They are not on public display, but I was permitted to read the letters when I visited Nuneaton during the research for this biography.

Larry clearly felt very comfortable with Pauline as a correspondent, because he always updated her with any changes of address, and he goes into often quite personal details about his health, holidays he's taken, work he's been asked to do, etc. He also chats about Fan, Barry his driver, the poodles, and of course the weather. The letters reflect some of Larry's very human fickle changes of heart. In June 1976 he reports his and Fan's great sadness at one of the poodles passing away, and he tells Pauline he'll never have another dog. In December of the same year he writes to tell her about the new poodle pup he has just bought. Similarly in September 1988 Larry writes to tell Pauline about the last stage show he is about to do before he retires completely from theatre work. In July 1993 he tells her about the music hall style show he has just starred in at The Norwich Theatre Royal.

The letters are usually newsy, bright and breezy, and always contain thoughtful questions about Pauline and her son, offering them support and congratulations for things they have done in their lives. Occasionally Larry confides great personal sadness, as in September 1989 when he poignantly tells Pauline that Fan has been taken into a nursing home.

One of the perks of stardom that Larry did enjoy was that it opened doors for him to meet some of his idols. He and Fan had always been big fans of the long-running daily soap opera *Crossroads*. They knew every character and followed all the plot twists avidly. Larry himself was a huge admirer of Noele Gordon, who played Meg Richardson, the owner of the motel. He believed Noele's screen presence equalled that of some of his most worshipped big screen goddesses from the golden days of Hollywood. I suppose at her most imperious she could be a bit 'Bette Davis'. Off-screen she certainly had the aura of a star about her, often making public appearances in furs and diamonds, waving regally at her fans from her sleek grey chauffeur-driven Rolls Royce with its personalised number plate NG 10.

Larry would always try to sneak a funny but endearing reference to *Crossroads* into all his television appearances in those early days, so he was thrilled when the manager of The Cresta Theatre Club in Solihull came into his dressing room one night to say that there was a big party in the audience from the cast of *Crossroads*. The only disappointment was that it didn't include Noele Gordon. After the cabaret show Maggie French, the production manager who worked for ATV on *Crossroads*, came round to Larry's dressing room to say how much they had all enjoyed his show. Larry impressed her with his encyclopaedic knowledge of the soap, so she half-jokingly asked him if he'd ever thought of being in it. He joined in the joke and said he'd love to walk into that famous reception and meet 'madam', as he laughingly called Noele Gordon.

Imagine his surprise when he received a phone call from ATV a couple of days later asking if he was serious about making a guest appearance in *Crossroads*. Of course he happily accepted a cameo role, which turned out to be as outrageously hilarious as his act. They told him his unlikely part was that of a back-packer who had been camping in a nearby field when torrential rain made him fold up his tent and check into The Crossroads Motel. Already fed up about his ruined camping holiday, he was going to complain to Meg Richardson about his night in her motel.

They perhaps foolishly left it to him to extemporise his complaints, so Noele Gordon only had a very rough idea of what he was going to say when they rolled tape to record the scene, which was in fact to be the last scene of that particular episode. They had only just met, so Noele had no clue what Larry was like. Expecting a brief but terse complaint back she gave him his cue, which was a simple "Good morning"... and Larry was off... "It may be a good morning for you, but I didn't get a wink of sleep all night! The chalet was dripping with water. I even found two fish in the bath! Then I tripped over Amy Turtle's bucket... Twice! Goodness only knows what that was doing sticking out from under my bed! I would have been better off staying where I was, rubbing two sticks together, trying to light a fire under my dixie. At least it would have kept me warm. I shivered all night in that Chalet 13!"

Noele was so stunned by this unexpected diatribe that she didn't deliver her scripted polite response, so Larry jumped back in again. The *Crossroads* production team had told Larry that Noele had recently received a very strange fan letter from a ferret-lover who wanted to "walk her out to the pictures". She'd politely replied that no woman should come between a man and his ferrets. Knowledge of this amusing exchange gave Larry his second wind: "And another thing Mrs Richardson! All night there has been gnawing and scratching at the woodwork! ... Have you got ferrets at this motel?"

It was a high risk strategy with an actress he didn't know, and who he held in such high esteem. She could have been furious, and he was hoping to make a friend of her. Noele Gordon's eyes glazed for a moment, ever the professional, knowing that the credits would be rolling over their silent face-off, after Larry's rant. As the director shouted "Cut!" Noele spluttered "You bastard!", then collapsed into an armchair and laughed helplessly. Eventually she got herself back under control, stood up, put her arms around Larry, and said: "I love you! I love you!". The whole studio erupted in laughter and applause. I don't suppose the *Crossroads* set had too many moments quite like that...

That was the start of an enduring friendship between the two of them, and they appeared on stage and on screen together many times after that day. Larry even made another cameo appearance on *Crossroads* in 1975 as Noele's uniformed chauffeur of the white Rolls Royce which was used for the wedding scenes on the day her character married to become Meg Mortimer. She wisely didn't let him speak this time. The irony was that Larry couldn't drive, even though it was his Rolls Royce that was used for the filming, with him sitting behind the wheel.

Larry had never had the inclination, or indeed the aptitude to learn to drive, but Peter Dulay had insisted that he should buy a Rolls Royce when he became a big star, as a status symbol. Larry had said "What's the good of that? I can't drive!" Dulay's answer was simple – get yourself a chauffeur. Encouraged by his new friend Noele Gordon, who told Larry he had earned himself a bit of luxury after scraping by for so many years, he did buy a white Rolls Royce, but he always sat in the front seat next to his driver, because he would have felt far too grand sitting in the back. "I'm not The Queen of the May!" he would say. Larry enjoyed the trappings of fame and stardom, after all his struggles, but he never became flashy or flamboyant. One of his friends was amused to find that Larry kept salt and vinegar in the glove compartment of the chauffeur-driven Rolls in case he fancied fish and chips after a performance.

Larry did enjoy the idea of having a male companion in the shape of a chauffeur however. He had several over the years, and of course he always chose good-looking younger men. It must have done his ego good to be seen accompanied by these strapping eye-catching fellows, and there is no doubt he enjoyed their company. It seems the relationships were perfectly innocent, but I feel sure that Larry got a kick out of having a young handsome man to look after him and with whom to share the long boring hours on the road, which is normally the least attractive part of being a touring comedian.

In 1973 Thames Television contacted Larry to invite him to be a guest on Noele Gordon's *This Is Your Life*. He remembered fondly how much the big red book treatment had meant to him, so he was keen to be a part of this fitting tribute to his dear friend. The only problem was that he was already booked to do late night cabaret at The Wakefield Theatre Club, so a fast car had to be on stand-by to whisk him back to Yorkshire right after the TV recording.

That evening in February 1973, during the recording of Noele's *This Is Your Life*, a rather odd rumour was born. Tabloid stories started to appear about a real life romance, and even possible wedding plans between Larry Grayson and Noele Gordon. The moment that started the rumour mill going into overdrive was Larry's appearance as the last surprise guest. Noele knew Larry was booked to appear in Wakefield that night, so she simply couldn't believe he was there when he walked through the door on to the studio set. She was literally rendered speechless for a moment as she stood staring at him in disbelief, so Larry broke the slightly awkward silence by looking into her eyes and saying: "Noele, I do love you!", to which she replied: "And I love you...". Having recovered from the shock of seeing Larry so unexpectedly, Noele turned to the audience and said: "I keep asking him to marry me, but he won't!". Larry quickly countered with: "Well I will then!". Swept away by the fun of it all Noele said: "Well you've said it now, and millions of viewers have heard you..."

Of course it was all said in a jokey way, in the heat of the moment between two genuinely close friends, but the press decided to take it seriously. Both Noele and Larry realised that they had opened Pandora's Box when they were inundated with congratulations cards and telegrams, flowers, gifts, and hundreds of phone calls from well-wishers, asking if they had set a date for the wedding. Years later Larry said that perhaps they shouldn't have joked about something so serious, but Noele reassured him that no real harm had been done as they really were great friends, even if they weren't engaged.

At the time Larry made capital from the situation on stage. He'd say things like: "I went to see the doctor this morning for a check-up. He said everything was in perfect working order... Noele Gordon will be pleased...".

In mid-October 1974 Larry had the great honour of having his face and his name up in lights outside The London Palladium. He was topping the bill at long last – twice nightly for six weeks. I began this book with his emotional phone call to Fan when he saw the front of the theatre for the first time. The show was aptly called *Grayson's Scandals*, and of course there was a special guest star – Noele Gordon, who sang, danced and happily joined in the comedy 'schtick' with Larry.

Noele did the show because Larry had asked her personally, even though it seemed out of character for her. In fact she had started out as a theatre performer, and the stage was really her first love, but she had done so much television in recent years that she was terribly nervous on the first night, stepping out in front of a large expectant Palladium audience. It had been fifteen years since she last 'trod the boards'. Larry reassured her and helped her through her first night nerves, but after that she loved every minute of it. It was a punishing schedule for Noele however, because she was in Birmingham during the day recording *Crossroads*, then being driven down the motorway for two evening performances with Larry at The London Palladium, then back again to Birmingham in the wee small hours, learning her lines for the following day in the studio. She was nearly always accompanied by her mother 'Jockey' on her lengthy commute between jobs. They were almost inseparable.

In that show, with a lot of the audience still happily believing that they were 'an item', Larry would take the mickey unmercifully out of his 'betrothed'. He'd complain that Noele was ever so old ("They make her up to look younger!"), deaf as a post, and could hardly walk any more, and then he'd make jokes about her being a big drinker ("Even dips her bread in it!"). The outrageous and of course untrue comments brought the house down every night, but Larry thought his world had come tumbling down when he received a writ from Noele Gordon's lawyers at the end of the run, claiming that "the plaintiff has been greatly injured in her character, credit and reputation". It went on to claim that Larry's nightly jibes had brought her into "public scandal, contempt and ridicule". It even listed all the unkind and untrue things he had said about her: "She is old... She is as deaf as a post... She is lame and can hardly walk... She drinks..."

Poor Larry broke into a cold sweat thinking that his dear friend was about to sue him for everything he'd struggled so hard to earn. After a while the penny slowly dropped. It was thankfully an elaborate and quite expensive prank – Noele's sweet revenge for the way Larry had ambushed her on the *Crossroads* set. Once he had recovered from the shock and realised it was thankfully just a joke, Larry had the legal writ, which had been drawn up by a genuine barrister, framed and he hung it on the wall at home.

Strangely, despite Larry's immense popularity at that time, the Palladium run hadn't done great business at the box office, and wasn't financially successful. *Grayson's Scandals* went on to do extremely well as a summer season stage show in various seaside resorts over the next few years, so it must have been a 'London thing'. London audiences can be mercurial to say the least. The promoters could obviously see potential in the provinces, because they asked Larry and Noele to take the show on tour around Britain. They were both keen on the idea, but Noele felt she had to say no in the end, out of loyalty to ATV and *Crossroads*. It was a decision she told Larry she bitterly regretted years later when ATV sacked her so callously from *Crossroads*. So much for loyalty.

Larry and Noele didn't appear to actively encourage the rumour about their so-called romance, but neither of them did very much to dispel it either. Of course the smokescreen may well have suited them both. While the press were asking about engagement rings and wedding plans they weren't asking Larry about other aspects of his personal life, and Noele could also avoid public scrutiny, which was very convenient as she'd always had a penchant for other women's husbands. There were persistent rumours that Noele herself was gay, presumably because she'd never married and was never photographed with a male partner. She certainly enjoyed the company of gay men, and perhaps was something of a gay icon, but nevertheless I have it on good authority from people who knew her well that her liaisons were all of a heterosexual nature. Apparently the reason she never married herself was that she had a 'thing' for powerful married men. It is well documented that she had a long-standing and quite public affair with showbusiness impresario Val Parnell, in full view of his wife Helen, and in fact with her blessing. Parnell, the old charmer, in the end dumped both his wife Helen and his mistress Noele Gordon in favour of a much younger woman, singer Aileen Cochrane.

The Larry / Noele marriage myth lingered for four years before they started to deny it. Even in 1977 Larry was still saying: "I don't know whether we'll ever get married, but she's always telling me how much she loves me". In the same interview he made the defensive remark that makes one wince to read it now: "Incidentally there's no reason why I shouldn't get married. Let me put it straight – I am not strange in any way... But I am a camp comedian and I do act that way. That's the great difference." In another ill-advised press interview, around the same time, Larry said: "I'm not really a queer or a homosexual. I'm just behaving like one. That's the difference." Sadly it was the language of the day, but they were unfortunate remarks that must have alienated quite a few of his many gay fans.

Gay friends and admirers of Larry have said that his big mistake was denying being gay. They say he didn't have to admit anything or 'come out', but he could have just declined to comment on his personal life and his sexuality. It was perhaps foolish, insensitive, and arguably almost offensive to pretend to be a heterosexual who had never found the right girl. His friend Danny La Rue had done the exact same thing. Personally I can sympathise a little as they had both had to find a way to survive through a time of cruel and vindictive intolerance. However I'm not really in a position to make judgments either way, or to fully understand how his denial was perceived by the gay community, as I am not gay myself, and I haven't had to cope with the problems Larry faced on a daily basis.

Larry's close friendship with 'Nolly' Gordon was real enough, and he was genuinely heartbroken when she lost the battle with stomach cancer in 1985, at the age of just sixty-five. She had never really recovered from the bitter blow of being sacked by ATV and written out of *Crossroads* in 1981, after seventeen years of loyal service to the programme. Larry always blamed the onset of cancer on the trauma of her sacking, compounded by the heartbreak of losing her beloved mother 'Jockey'. Noele had spoken to Larry from her hospital bed a couple of days before she died, but he hadn't realised just how close to the end she was. He was too upset to talk to journalists when he first heard Nolly had passed away, but a few days later he tearfully paid tribute to his dear friend in glowing terms, and of course attended her funeral as 'chief mourner'.

THEATRE ROYAL, BRIGHTON
PAUL ELLIOTT & DUNCAN C. WELDON present
DORA BRYAN
in The HOWARD & WYNDHAM Pantomime
GOLDILOCKS and the THREE BEARS
BOBBY DENNIS
LARRY GRAYSON
RAY CHIARELLA · OLIVIA BREEZE
From BILLY SMART'S CIRCUS
THE ROBERTIS
and GWYN The International Trapeze Artist
VALENTINE DYALL
Directed by JOHN DE LANNOY
Choreography by SUE ADDAMS
Musical Direction by WILL FYFFE JR.

FESTIVAL THEATRE
PAIGNTON TEL 58641/2
OPENS THURSDAY JUNE 10th
6·0 TWICE NIGHTLY 8·30
PRICES 85p 75p 60p 40p
LESLIE GRADE & BERNARD DELFONT present
LESLIE CROWTHER
Crowther's in Town!
T.V.'s BASIL BRUSH
PIERRE BEL
SHEILA BERNETTE
LAURI LUPINO LANE
LARRY GRAYSON
PETER HUGHES
TOMMY SHAW DANCERS
EDDIE CONNOR
PRODUCED BY ALBERT J. KNIGHT
SPECIAL GUEST STAR!
DESERT SONG
STUDENT PRINCE
VAGABOND KING
JOHN HANSON
THE ROMANTIC SINGING STAR OF WEST END MUSICALS AND TELEVISION

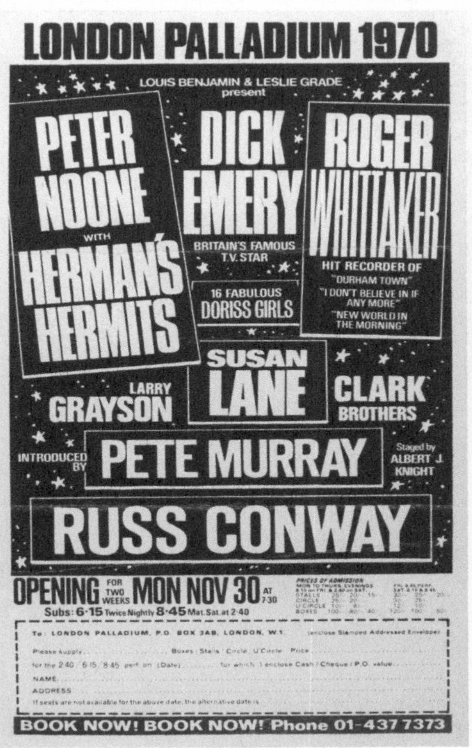
LONDON PALLADIUM 1970
LOUIS BENJAMIN & LESLIE GRADE present
PETER NOONE
WITH
HERMAN'S HERMITS
DICK EMERY
BRITAIN'S FAMOUS T.V. STAR
ROGER WHITTAKER
HIT RECORDER OF "DURHAM TOWN" "I DON'T BELIEVE IN IF ANY MORE" "NEW WORLD IN THE MORNING"
16 FABULOUS DORISS GIRLS
LARRY GRAYSON
SUSAN LANE
CLARK BROTHERS
INTRODUCED BY
PETE MURRAY
Staged by ALBERT J. KNIGHT
RUSS CONWAY
OPENING FOR TWO WEEKS MON NOV 30 AT 7·30
Subs: 6·15 Twice Nightly 8·45 Mat. Sat. at 2·40
To: LONDON PALLADIUM, P.O. BOX 3AB, LONDON, W.1.
BOOK NOW! BOOK NOW! Phone 01-437 7373

THEATRE ROYAL
BRIGHTON
BERNARD DELFONT presents
BRIGHTON'S BIGGEST SHOW
KATHY KIRBY
ARTHUR ASKEY
STARTIME
HEATHMORE
SAVEEN
WITH DAISY MAY
MAURICE FOURNIER
JO COOK
SAXON LUCAS
LARRY GRAYSON
THE TELEVISION GO-JOS
including OLD TIME MUSIC HALL featuring
MISS HETTY KING

Above: In his element, on stage.

Below: Back in drag, with The Kaye Sisters.

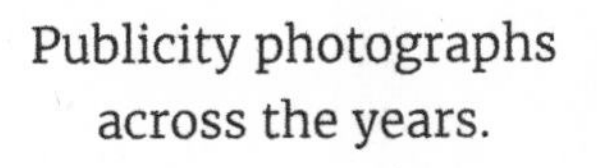

Publicity photographs
across the years.

Top: Larry's proudest moment, meeting The Queen at *The Royal Gala Show*, The London Palladium 1972.

Above and right: Larry with his silver screen idol Gracie Fields at the opening of The Gracie Fields Theatre in Rochdale, 1978. Group photo, left to right: Ben Warriss, Gracie Fields, Larry, Sandy Powell, agent Billy Marsh, Gracie's husband Boris Alperovici.

Larry with...

Clockwise from top left: Eric Morecambe; both Arthur Marshalls; Liberace; Isla St Clair; Danny la Rue and Isla St Clair; Noele Gordon.

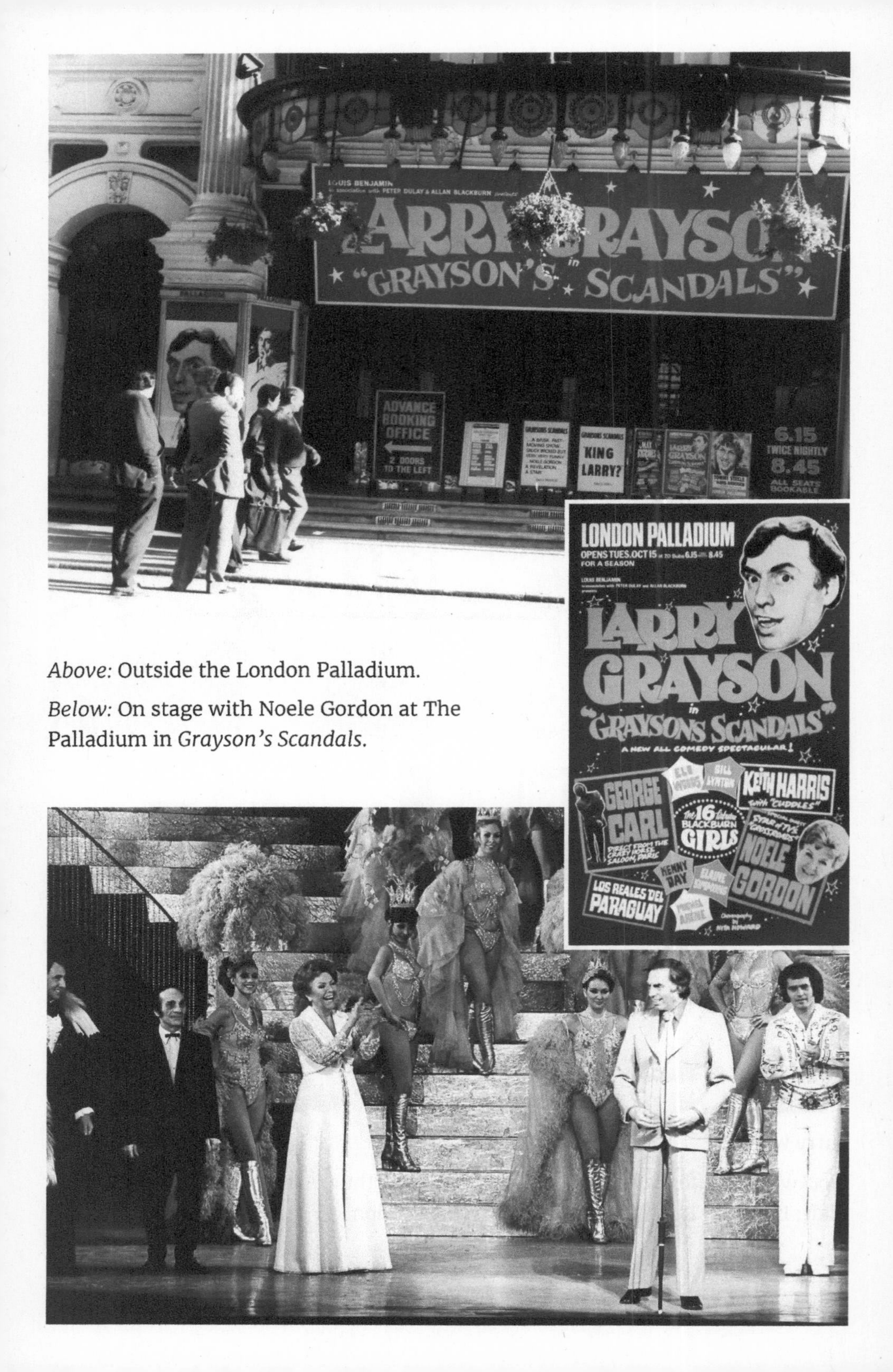

Above: Outside the London Palladium.

Below: On stage with Noele Gordon at The Palladium in *Grayson's Scandals*.

Above: On set in the *Crossroads* motel reception with Ann George and Noele Gordon.

Below: Noele Gordon and Larry clowning on the Palladium stage.

Below, left to right: Foster sister May's daughters Joan and Joyce, foster sister Fan, Larry and Arthur Marshall the poodle.

The woman Larry loved most in the world, foster sister Fan.

Above: Fan, Larry and William the poodle.

Below: The family grave in Oaston Road Cemetery, Nuneaton (bearing the wrong birth date for Alice).

12

... a love affair with The English Riviera...

In 1976 Larry began another long-term love affair, this time with a place. His show *Grayson's Scandals*, which had started life at The London Palladium with special guest star Noele Gordon, and had subsequently been a big hit (without Noele) in Margate and later Blackpool, was booked for the 1976 summer season at The Princess Theatre in Torquay. Because a summer season is such a long run, far from home, the performers all take 'digs' in the vicinity of the theatre. The size and quality of the rented digs obviously varies according to how high or low the performer is on the bill. As the star of the show Larry could now afford nicer accommodation, so he rented a big house on Ilsham Marine Drive, in a select eastern suburb of the resort.

He quickly discovered that he loved living on 'The English Riviera', as Torbay has named itself. He also discovered that it was home to people who he had worshipped from afar. Larry, Fan and their 'dad' Jim had always been big fans of the long-running country-folk BBC radio soap opera *The Archers*. Larry was excited to hear that Gwen Berryman, who had played Doris Archer from the very beginnings of the iconic series back in the early 1950s, lived in Torquay. He was even more excited when she came backstage after one performance to introduce herself. They struck up a warm friendship right away and remained friends until Gwen's death in 1983. Gwen was able to introduce Larry to other members of the cast of *The Archers*. Norman Painting, who played Phil Archer, became another close friend.

It was a very happy summer for Larry. He made lots of friends, and would hold regular parties in his big rented house. There was one regular visitor called Michael Parker, who was a young hairdresser, Butlins redcoat and fledgling comedian. He'd hang around the theatre, watching Larry work as often as he could, copying his mannerisms and style, and borrowing them for his own evolving act. Larry could see the young man's potential and told him he would be a star one day. Michael Parker changed his name to Michael Barrymore – you may have heard of him! Larry was very generous with people like Michael. He'd take them under his wing, and offer them encouragement. He'd been there – he knew what it is like to be a young struggling unknown, and he knew how much he owed to his guardian angels who had helped him along the way, so this was his way of giving something back, or "paying it forward" as the Americans say.

When Larry came to take over *The Generation Game* he really stuck his neck out for Barrymore. Alan Boyd, the producer, had an experienced warm-up comedian called Felix Bowness booked, never seen by viewers at home, but always on hand to keep the audience amused between takes and when the stage was being re-set. Larry insisted on Michael Barrymore being given the opportunity to do a couple of the shows as the warm-up comedian, against Boyd's better judgment. Larry then invited Jim Moir, the BBC Head Of Variety, to the BBC Television Theatre to see Michael warming up the audience. Moir was impressed enough to give Barrymore the odd spot on television, which helped launch him into the big time. This was very generous of Larry, especially as Barrymore was not the ideal type of comedian for keeping an audience warmed-up in a TV studio. Warm-up comics have to be quite low-key and know when to shut up. Barrymore failed on both counts.

On Sunday evenings, when there wasn't a show to perform, Larry would get his driver to take him into the country, away from the hustle and bustle and the tourists of Torquay. He found a cosy pub called 'The Artichoke Inn' in a village called Christow, where he could enjoy a quiet drink in peace. He'd fondly remembered the pub from his days touring the West Country in *Tomorrow's Stars*, nearly thirty years before, and was delighted to find it was still there, and hadn't been spoilt by the ravages of time. One Sunday evening in 'The Artichoke' he was chatting to one of the local ladies, who happened to casually mention that there was another famous person in the village. Larry's ears pricked up, still finding his own celebrity a novelty.

The lady said Larry probably wouldn't know of him, but his name was Arthur Marshall. Larry was thrilled. He had been a big fan of Arthur's since his wartime radio series *A Date with Nurse Dugdale*. Readers of a certain age might just remember Arthur as the opposing team captain to Frank Muir on the panel game about obscure words, *Call My Bluff*. He was a jolly, bespectacled, rotund little man with a whimsical, gentle sense of humour, an infectious chuckle and a seemingly permanent smile.

A few weeks later Larry was in Christow again and decided to ask one of the locals if they knew where Arthur Marshall lived. He was given directions down a long narrow lane to a beautiful archetypal English country cottage, the sort of picturesque little old place that was featured on jigsaws, picture postcards, biscuit tins and chocolate boxes in those days. The cottage was surrounded by a neatly trimmed hedge and overlooked an orchard, an idyllic English setting frozen in time, the only sound in the air was the bees buzzing around. It was simply charming, like something out of *The Darling Buds of May*.

Larry really just wanted to take a peep at 'Goose Cottage', where Marshall lived, so he was rather embarrassed when he suddenly heard Arthur's voice trill out: "Hello there. Can I help you?" Larry apologised profusely for the intrusion and started to explain who he was. He didn't need to do so. Arthur said: "Oh you're Larry Grayson! Do come in dear – I'll put the kettle on at once, we must have a cup of tea. I've just got back from Italy."

It turned out that Arthur was as big a fan of Larry as Larry was of Arthur. They got on like a house on fire, two naturally witty men with a lively sense of humour. Arthur was a great raconteur and Larry loved listening to his stories, then they'd fall about giggling at something and nothing. They were kindred spirits. Arthur was equally discreet about his sexuality, never speaking about it, but sharing his life and his country cottage with a retired schoolmaster. Arthur even shared Larry's love of classic films and The Golden Age of Hollywood. They remained extremely close friends until Arthur's death in 1989. For Larry finding Arthur Marshall must have been a bit like finding a reincarnation of his old school friend Tom Proctor.

It is a measure of how much Larry thought of Arthur that he named one of his three beloved pet poodles after him. Peter the poodle sadly died in the early part of Larry's 1976 summer season in Torquay, at the ripe old age of seventeen. Larry and Fan were very upset and Larry swore that they would never have another dog as it was so distressing when they died. By December of the same year he had relented and succumbed to buying a white poodle pup, which he christened 'Arthur Marshall'. Praise didn't come any greater than that in Larry's life.

With this new circle of fellow showbusiness professionals, the balmy climate of 'The English Riviera', and the genteel tranquillity of the Torbay area, Larry had found somewhere he loved being, almost more so than Nuneaton. With money suddenly coming in faster than he knew how to spend it, Larry invested in a luxury two-bedroom apartment with a sea view, on the upmarket eastern fringe of Torquay, in Thatcher Avenue. His showbiz neighbours included Cyril Fletcher and Freddie Starr. Larry became great friends with Cyril Fletcher and his wife Betty who had the penthouse flat at the top of the building. They would regularly pop in for coffee, or invite him up to see them.

Larry used his apartment as a bolthole where he could escape with friends for a few days when he wasn't working. Fan would often go with him, but home for both of them was still most definitely 'The Garlands' in Nuneaton. Larry wasn't a great one for foreign holidays, so Torquay was his way of getting away from it all, and was about as exotic as he was prepared to go. After his record breaking summer season with *Grayson's Scandals* at The Winter Gardens in Margate he had decided to treat himself to a luxury cruise, but he cancelled it at the last minute, because he said he'd already had enough sun in Margate. He did take occasional foreign holidays, but didn't always enjoy them. As a big treat he took himself off to Hawaii once, but hated every minute of it. Larry simply wasn't cut out to be a daring globetrotter, preferring simple English home-cooked food and the familiarity of good old Blighty.

Larry's love affair with Torquay would eventually turn sour, as many love affairs do, but for now the apartment there was his one real reward to himself for finally making it as a star. It was somewhere he could relax and enjoy life to the full.

In 1973, with two successful series of *Shut That Door* under his belt, Larry, his manager Peter Dulay and the ATV production team started work on developing his stage title *Grayson's Scandals* for television. Unfortunately ATV, the company who had given Larry his big break, couldn't guarantee that this new series would be shown at the same time all over the ITV network. Peter Dulay took umbrage and thought this was an intolerable way for such a big star to be treated. Dulay fell out with Lew Grade over ATV's perceived lack of commitment to his most important client, strongly advising Larry not to go ahead with the series. Larry found the situation extremely uncomfortable. He had always hated confrontation of any sort, and was embarrassed by the fall-out with his employers, the company who had made him famous after all these years, but he told journalists that he always did what his manager advised him to do. Consequently *Grayson's Scandals* never did see the light of day on television, and the subsequent discord meant that there was nothing else on the cards for Larry at ATV.

It was a dangerous strategy on Dulay's part. Not many showbiz managers would have risked putting Lew Grade's nose out of joint – he was a very powerful man in British television at that time. This could have been a premature end to a very promising TV career. In fact, apart from the odd guest appearance, Larry was off our screens for over a year. Peter Dulay told the press that they were considering offers from the BBC to jump channels, which was classic agent-speak for "we haven't got a clue what he's going to do next", and a subtle way of letting the BBC know that Larry was available. Larry even started telling journalists that he would probably retire very soon, which again was panicky damage limitation during this uncertain time. Dulay quickly denied the retirement rumours as that was counter-productive for a star performer looking for a fresh start. He said Larry could never retire, being the sort of person who is such a born performer that he opens a fridge door and takes four bows because the light has come on.

Fortunately Lew Grade's nephew Michael Grade came to Larry's rescue once again. He was no longer an agent himself, but he had taken a job as deputy controller of programmes at London Weekend Television, in charge of their entertainment output. Michael was still a big fan of Larry's and knew him well, having been his agent. So, when he discovered that Larry was very much available and no longer working for Uncle Lew, he snatched him up and signed him to make a one hour special for LWT called *The Larry Grayson Hour of Stars*. London Weekend Television had a stranglehold on the national ITV weekend schedule in those days, so Peter Dulay got his guarantee of the show being seen by the entire ITV network on the evening of Friday 13th September 1974, although in the end that didn't actually happen. Lew Grade's ATV and one other ITV region decided to show it a few days earlier. Perhaps Uncle Lew was flexing his not inconsiderable TV muscle and trying to create a ratings spoiler. He was certainly a dangerous man to cross at that time. Nevertheless it was seen by virtually the whole ITV network that week.

Larry was in his element with this lavish special, as the theme of the show was classic cinema and The Golden Age of Hollywood. He was now a big enough name to attract major stars to appear with him. Michael Crawford was one of the main guests, but Larry must have been even more thrilled about his other star guest that night, Dame Anna Neagle. Larry had worshipped her from afar in all her many screen roles throughout his formative cinema-going years. He admitted he was terribly nervous of meeting her, and you can see he is genuinely in awe of her as she walks on to the set. He couldn't have been more reverential if he'd been granted a private audience with The Queen. In fact Dame Anna's performance is so stiff and regal it almost appears as though it is exactly that.

The Larry Grayson Hour of Stars was, in my personal opinion, a little disappointing. The Hollywood theme seemed purely to pander to Larry's obsession with classic cinema, and felt self-indulgent and quite outdated, even for its time. The admittedly spectacular and lavishly produced show didn't particularly play to Larry's strengths either. He wasn't much of a song and dance man, and both Michael Crawford and Dame Anna Neagle appeared purely as interview guests. Larry was not at his best as a chat show host. The fawning interviews seem almost embarrassingly sycophantic, as he continually tells them both how marvellous they are. I'm sure his adoration was sincere, but it makes oddly uncomfortable viewing.

Presumably the idea of guests being interviewed by Larry had come from *Shut That Door*, where he would occasionally invite showbiz pals along to chat about the good old days – the likes of Dora Bryan, Leslie Crowther, Diana Dors and of course Noele Gordon. Larry got away with this reasonably well because they just gossiped away like old friends do. However, when it came to major stars he'd never met before, he was definitely no Michael Parkinson. Nevertheless the one-off *Larry Grayson Hour of Stars* was perceived as successful enough to warrant Michael Grade and London Weekend Television giving Larry an eponymous ITV series.

The simply titled *Larry Grayson* ran for two seasons, one in late 1975, transmitting on Friday evenings, followed by another seven episodes in early 1977, which transmitted within the much-coveted Saturday night ITV entertainment schedule. In series one Larry was back in his comfort zone with a format that suited him much better than the special he'd made. It was a simple cocktail of high camp gossipy stand-up comedy; sketches where he could basically play a version of himself, alongside guest actors;

and performance guests with whom he could have a bit of fun – the likes of Rod Hull and Emu, stage sharp-shooters, acrobats, knife throwers and magicians. Series two followed a similar pattern, kicking off with a one hour special, with more star guests, but the same familiar mix of variety acts, sketches and Larry's inimitable stand-up / sit-down comedy, plus the addition of a bit of padding in the shape of star singing guests. London Weekend Television were masters at this type of glitzy variety / comedy show and *Larry Grayson* was a huge success.

Larry was never great with a script. He had always had trouble remembering jokes and he wasn't very good at learning lines. You can see in some of the sketches a look of panic flash into the eyes of the other guest actors because Larry has wandered off the script, or he has forgotten what he is supposed to say, and they aren't quite sure where to go next, not having received their correct cue. Larry never looks flustered however, because he could always ad lib his way out of such a situation, even if it was just a look to camera to give them time to find their way back into the script, roughly as they had rehearsed it. In that way the sketch or routine always seems to get salvaged. He can't have been easy to work with though. I think for actors that is about as close as they get to living life on the edge. Actors working with the unpredictable and ill-disciplined Tommy Cooper suffered similar problems, but it does make great television for the viewers and, after all, that is what it's all about.

During this period of national fame and high earnings Larry, as one might expect, attracted an entourage of hangers-on and camp followers. Two men, who both worshipped Larry, but tended to snipe at one another, took to travelling with him everywhere in the back of the chauffeur-driven Rolls Royce – Peter Smith and Barry Young. Peter would claim that he was Larry's road manager, and then Barry would say: "You're not his road manager, I am!" Larry would snap: "Neither of you are my road manager – just sit in the back and shut up about it!". I wondered why an astute man like Larry put up with them being around, and sponging off him, but the simple truth was that they made him laugh, and he enjoyed their company. He also couldn't resist teasing them and gently making fun of their outrageous camp appearance and ways. Larry often referred to them, behind their backs of course, as "The Uglies", short for "Ugly Sisters". Paul Vaughan says that whilst they both loved basking in the reflected glory of their famous acquaintance, Barry was more inclined to use Larry for his own ends, whereas Peter was more of a loyal friend, and made himself useful when they went anywhere. Larry enjoyed telling friends that he now had a 'personal assistant'.

Larry's television comeback had put him back in demand on other shows. In 1977 he made guest appearances on a couple of episodes of Bob Monkhouse's *Celebrity Squares*, and he was asked to star in an edition of the BBC's *The Good Old Days*, a personal favourite of Larry's. Recorded in the small but lovingly preserved Leeds City Varieties Theatre, with the audience and participants all in period costume, the long-running variety series harked back to the heyday of old time music hall. Larry was completely at home on that show, and would publicly mourn its passing when *The Good Old Days* was axed in 1983.

Having thoroughly enjoyed his late blossoming fame throughout the 1970s, it was towards the end of that happy decade that a dark cloud began to loom on the horizon. Larry started having trouble with the increasingly vocal 'Gay Liberation Front', and other gay activists. At one of the early Gay Pride marches a large banner read: "Laugh at Larry Grayson and you're laughing at us". One marcher told the press: "As far as we are concerned they don't come much lower than Larry Grayson". Peter Tatchell, one of the leading British campaigners for gay rights, said at the time: "Quentin Crisp, along with Larry Grayson and John Inman, confirm rather than challenge prejudices." In 1978 the newspaper 'Gay News' described Larry's appointment as the new Generation Game host as: "... the worst possible thing that could happen to gay rights on television...", adding later: "... he will earn many thousands of pounds at our expense. He will become a 'superstar' while he confuses and distresses our teenage brothers...". Speaking to Julian Clary, who was himself a gay teenager at that time, he assured me that certainly wasn't the case in his experience. He looked up to Larry as a role model.

Much as Larry would have liked to bury his head in the sand and ignore them, he couldn't really avoid the right of response when journalists asked him how he felt about his gay critics and their strong condemnation. In a rare moment of losing his usual calm composure in front of the cameras, Larry snarled back with equal contempt: "Gay?! I've never seen a more serious, miserable lot in my life!" He hated being labelled 'gay' himself, saying: "I am what I am. It's just me!". Jean Rook, an intelligent journalist and columnist for the *Daily Express*, immediately leapt to Larry's defence, which was surprising as both Ms Rook and her newspaper were Conservative with a capital 'C'. She had asked to interview Larry at The Savoy Hotel. He'd agreed, but was terrified of the prospect, as she had a pretty fearsome reputation. However she put him at his ease as soon as they met by saying: "Don't worry. I like you."

In her newspaper piece she said: "The almost total heterosexual acceptance of Grayson's high camp should be a gay day for homosexuals. Laugh and the world laughs with you – and if it doesn't see it your way, it may at least view you with a more tolerant eye." She also said: "At a flop of the wrist Larry Grayson has done more for Gay Liberation than a full scale Hyde Park rally to their cause. He's legalised camp, playfully knocked over sex barriers, taught women to laugh, and men not to sneer." She saw his rise to fame as a powerful symbol of popular tolerance. Perhaps easy to say when you are a heterosexual woman.

It is hard to recall the single-minded righteous fury of pressure groups in those days, even for somebody like me, who was around at the time. It was a time of revolution to overthrow bigotry and intolerance. There was real and justified worldwide anger about women's rights, racial equality, and now gay rights. Wars had to be won, even if it meant a few casualties along the way. I feel history has been kinder to Larry, and many gay people now remember him fondly as an influence, a pioneer and perhaps even an inspiration.

I am in grave danger of falling into the same trap as Jean Rook if I express an opinion, but I do know that Larry was exactly the same off-stage and on, so he definitely wasn't camping it up to mock gay people. He really was saying: "I am what I am – take it or leave it", and I think it was probably a good thing that the vast majority of the British population chose to take it, and embraced him for it. He didn't set out to be a crusader, he only wanted to entertain, but I think he may well have inadvertently spear-headed a more tolerant attitude in Britain towards gay men.

Larry's only mistake, if you can call it that, was publicly denying being gay himself. If he'd been a politician or a heartthrob that might have been more acceptable and understandable, but as his entire act relied upon people believing that he was gay, you can see why his denials caused some offence to those who were trying to demystify homosexuality and allow gay people to emerge from the shadows. It would be a bit like Billy Connolly pretending not to be Scottish – the Scots would have some justification for feeling betrayed by him.

According to Paul Vaughan Larry didn't so much want to deny his sexuality as disassociate and distance himself from the promiscuous gay culture of the time. Larry genuinely didn't approve of any form of promiscuity. The last thing he wanted was to be linked with some of the gay celebrity headlines of the time, regarding the likes of Freddie Mercury, Boy George and Kenny Everett.

It got to the point where large groups of gay activists were actually picketing theatres where Larry was appearing. They even picketed The BBC Television Theatre in Shepherds Bush one night when they were recording an episode of *Larry Grayson's Generation Game.* They made such a noise outside in the street that the recording had to be stopped, and a flustered producer sent Larry's manager, Paul Vaughan, outside to sort out the problem. Understandably Paul was not experienced at pacifying an angry mob, but he decided to invite the ringleaders to meet Larry and say what they had to say to him in person. They agreed to remain quiet enough for the show to be completed, then a couple of them were escorted to Larry's dressing room.

Larry warmly welcomed them, then asked: "So what's all this about then?" They said they wanted him to admit that he was homosexual. His eyebrows shot up in horror and he clasped his hands over his little dog's ears, saying: "You can't use that word in here – it frightens my poodle!" They did laugh fortunately, and in the end his disarming natural charm won them over, and an uneasy truce was declared. It was a stalemate though, not a victory on either side.

A similar thing happened outside a theatre in Lewisham, where a crowd of protesters from The Lewisham Campaign for Homosexual Equality formed a noisy picket line. Among them was the late Paul Patrick, a prominent gay rights campaigner. Paul had previously written a letter to Larry, saying that he was not the object of their complaint, it was rather that the media only allowed one image of a gay man - his - to appear on screen, therefore distorting the reality of their lives.

Once again Paul Vaughan approached the protesters with all good grace and invited Paul Patrick and a couple of the other key figures backstage after the show to meet Larry. Patrick admitted he was surprised to find that Larry was "a kind, gentle man with a fine intelligence, great warmth and a sharp wit". A thoughtful discussion ensued where they say he readily admitted to them that he was indeed gay, but he reminded them that he was a mere entertainer and that, as such, he was in no position to fight for a cause, and had no appetite to be a crusader. Slowly, as Larry told them about his life and career, they began to realise the prejudices and abuse he'd had to face in some of the tough venues he'd played in much less tolerant times. Paul Patrick, an intelligent man, could suddenly see how the denials and public smokescreens had been born out of necessity, rather than a snub to fellow gay men. Years later Paul Patrick, writing about Larry's legacy, said: "I never thought I would have become one of Grayson's champions. But I am, and proud to be so!"

Gay academic, media lecturer and writer Andy Medhurst also came round to publicly acknowledging the debt that camp culture owed to Larry Grayson. Revering him as a gay icon and camp role model, he admits Larry was: "... once the most unjustly vilified of English queer comedians". Medhurst is referring here to Larry's vilification by the militant gay community, not the general public. He praises Larry's central and historic role in bringing camp into the mass media, and making it widely acceptable to the public at large, pointing out the importance of 'camp' to many gay men and its reclaimed acceptance in modern gay culture.

These tricky confrontations were part of the price of fame, but Larry found there were a lot of plusses to being famous as well. Money never seemed to be a driving force for him. He had always been perfectly content in the terraced house with no car. He just loved the business he was in. That doesn't mean to say that he didn't enjoy having a few quid in the bank, but stardom gave him much more than that – things that money just can't buy. He took immense pleasure from privileged celebrity moments, like being introduced to The Queen and Prince Philip for example, and also meeting his idols. In 1978 Larry had what he described as one of the biggest thrills of his life.

Billy Marsh, one of the top showbiz agents at the time, phoned Larry to say that Gracie Fields was going back to her home town of Rochdale to perform at the opening of a new theatre, named in her honour. Billy told Larry that he was one of the few acts of sufficient stature to introduce Gracie on to the stage. He was diplomatically asking Larry to take a step back from headlining his own shows and being second on the bill once again, but this was for Gracie Fields. In Larry's eyes British stars didn't come any better or any bigger, so being her support act was truly a great honour. He had of course seen every film she had ever made, and he had been a huge fan of hers ever since her chirpy cheeky sense of humour and distinctive singing voice had lifted the nation's spirits in the dark depressed times of his childhood in the 1930s. Sitting in The Scala Picture House in Nuneaton, watching Gracie up there on the silver screen he couldn't have imagined that over forty years later he would be sharing a stage with the great lady herself. It was beyond his wildest dreams to think he'd ever meet such a big star, never mind be on the same bill as her.

Also on the bill on that special gala opening night of The Gracie Fields Theatre was the wonderful old comedian Sandy Powell, Ben Warriss, The Rochdale Town Band, and The Rochdale Choir. Larry opened the second half with a twenty-minute spot, some of which was especially tailored to suit the occasion. After he took his bows he was quite emotional when he said: "Ladies and gentlemen, in my showbusiness career I have always longed to be invited to say just three words. Tonight, at long last, I am privileged to do just that... Miss Gracie Fields!".

The eighty-year-old grand dame walked out from the wings and the entire theatre rose to their feet, cheering and clapping. Larry said it was one of the most magical moments of his entire life. He stood in the wings and watched as she entranced the appreciative packed house with all her old hit songs, having to occasionally hush the excited crowd with the words: "Now listen. I can't hear myself think! I'm going deaf in one ear, and daft in the other..." In the opposite wing Larry could see Gracie's husband Boris watching, equally spellbound, and still obviously very much in love with his remarkable wife. It was one of her last ever public appearances as she sadly died the following year, having been made Dame Gracie Fields just seven months before her passing. Larry never forgot her though, or that special night.

13

... the scores on the doors... at the top of his game...

In 1978 Bruce Forsyth shocked his BBC bosses by walking away from his massive hit series *The Generation Game*. He had signed a contract with Michael Grade at London Weekend Television, where he was to have the whole of the highly prestigious autumn Saturday night ITV schedule handed over to him for the mammoth production *Bruce Forsyth's Big Night*. This left the BBC with a huge problem. Firstly they were losing one of the country's most popular names in entertainment to the opposition. Secondly he would be competing head-on against them on Saturday nights, where the BBC had traditionally ruled the roost, in no small part thanks to Brucie himself. Thirdly they were in danger of losing one of their most successful game show formats. Bruce had made *The Generation Game* his own, and it was almost felt that he was unique in the role of host and therefore irreplaceable.

Corporate hands were wrung and creative heads were scratched. The only other person who had ever hosted the show in Britain was Roy Castle who had filled in one Saturday night in 1975 when Bruce was ill, and had made a good job of the show at extremely short notice. Inevitably Roy's was the first name suggested as a possible replacement for Bruce, as he had already proved he had all the necessary skills. He was seriously considered for the suddenly vacant full-time role, but, being a similar all-round entertainer, Roy Castle would inevitably have been directly judged against the former host. The show's producer Alan Boyd believed that the only way to reinvent the series successfully was to have a complete contrast to Forsyth, somebody where direct comparisons were virtually impossible.

Lots of names were thrown around, but it was the show's astute and talented Programme Associate, comedy writer Tony Hawes, who suggested the name Larry Grayson to Alan Boyd. It was a completely off-the-wall suggestion but, as it turns out, an inspired one. Alan thought it was an interesting enough idea to arrange a trip with Tony Hawes to Great Yarmouth where Larry was appearing on The Wellington Pier in his perennial summer show *Grayson's Scandals*. They watched the show and both agreed that Larry certainly was good with people, and was definitely not from the same mould as *The Generation Game*'s outgoing host, even though he was every bit as funny in his own unique way. Alan liked what he saw and went backstage after the show to talk to Larry about the vacancy.

Larry was never one of those ruthlessly ambitious performers who elbow others out of the way to get ahead, so he was quite languid about the idea of taking over this major flagship BBC1 show, rather to Alan Boyd's surprise. In fact it was quite endearing to be faced by somebody who wasn't pushy, and Alan and Tony found it amusing that Larry didn't seem to realise the enormity of what they were suggesting. Even though Larry knew the BBC were coming to talk to him he hadn't given this potentially giant life-changing career move any serious thought whatsoever. Nevertheless he didn't seem resistant to the idea either, so Boyd and Hawes went back to Television Centre in London with their first choice for the job firmly fixed in their minds. Like most people that met and worked with him they had taken to Larry Grayson the person, as well as Larry Grayson the performer.

The man in charge of BBC1 in those days was the legendary Bill Cotton, who had been personally responsible for many of the classic entertainment programmes of that golden period. In fact it was his masterstroke to put Brucie in charge of *The Generation Game* in the first place. Cotton had championed Roy Castle as he'd really been hoping for a 'like for like' replacement for Forsyth, so he expressed serious doubts about Larry as a suggestion, but Alan Boyd convinced him that what Larry lacked in game show expertise he more than made up for in charm, humanity, hilarity and likeability. In the end Bill relented and gave Alan the go-ahead to make a pilot with Larry to see how it worked out.

When he was first made a serious offer Larry wasn't convinced that he was right for the role either. He told the BBC bosses he wasn't sure whether he was more like Bruce Forsyth, or his glamorous co-host Anthea Redfern. Alan Boyd said they didn't want him to be either Bruce or Anthea – they just wanted him to be himself. That was enough to convince Larry to give it a try. That and a phone call to Helen Edden, aka Madame Credo, his clairvoyant friend, who read his cards and predicted the show would be a big hit for him.

He always said that he didn't take the job for the money, and, at the age of fifty-five he wasn't really ambitious any more, but *The Generation Game* was such a big prestigious show, it was flattering to be offered it, too flattering to turn down in fact. It was high risk for everybody. If he failed the BBC would look very foolish, Larry's career would suffer, and London Weekend Television / ITV would rub their hands together with glee.

The more Alan Boyd spoke to Larry about the show, the more he realised that his new host was going to need help with the logistics and mechanics of the game itself. The answer was to avoid the fashionable game show trend for a glamorous blonde dippy sidekick, and cast a quick-thinking female co-host for Larry, who wasn't just a 'trolley-dolly', or a bit of 'eye-candy', but rather a smart young woman who could quietly take control when needed. Again many names were suggested and considered, but none seemed quite right.

One evening Alan Boyd was visiting his mother and sick father in Edinburgh and happened to switch on the TV for a local late night Scottish magazine programme, which was hosted by a bright bubbly twenty-six-year-old folk singer and actress called Isla St Clair, real name Isabella Margaret Dyce. Alan liked what he saw and could tell that Isla had already mastered the complexities of appearing natural in front of a television camera. He contacted her agent immediately and a test was arranged to see if the 'chemistry' was there between Larry and Isla. He promised Larry that if he didn't take to Isla, no more would be said, and they would look elsewhere. Larry did like her however. Isla's attractive but likable homely girl-next-door appeal made her the perfect foil for Grayson, a role in which a busty, leggy blonde could never have worked. Alan Boyd described Isla to me as a Julie Andrews type. I can see what he means, but I think more Mary Poppins than Maria – capable and reliable, with the ability to be both skittish and schoolmarmish when either need arose.

Marcus Plantin, the director of the show, said it was a steep learning curve for Larry, as he'd never hosted a game show before, and had only ever been a variety artiste. He'd never been particularly well-versed in television discipline, even when he was making his own shows for ITV, so there were inevitably minor teething problems as they headed towards the pilot recording. Larry started to tell producer Alan Boyd that he didn't rehearse, to which Alan had to firmly say "Yes – you – do!". As he was cajoled into trying dummy runs of the various games Larry's lack of game show expertise became more and more evident, which of course made rehearsal even more essential. Larry's usual method of working – "Stick me in front of the camera and see what happens!" – wasn't going to suffice for such a heavily formatted show.

Alan Boyd decided to write all Larry's instructions on cards for him, but this immediately introduced another problem. To follow the cards Larry needed his reading glasses, then he'd whip his specs off again to carry on with the show. Alan told him that would make editing the show virtually impossible as he'd have his glasses on in one shot and not in the next – it would be a continuity nightmare. Larry promised that he would keep his spectacles on all the time. Of course the moment there were cameras watching vanity took over and off would come the offending specs for the close-up shots. Alan said, even with the glasses on the famous string around Larry's neck, continuity was always his video tape editor's biggest headache. Larry didn't much like the idea of contact lenses either, so it was a problem they just had to face and deal with. No doubt there was a lot of cursing and swearing in the edit suite.

The truth, as Marcus Plantin observed, was that Larry simply didn't understand the mechanics of making a television programme. He was a master stage performer with forty years of experience, but video tape editing, cameras and television trickery were a mystery to him, and something to be left to the experts.

One simple TV technique in the show which did appeal to Larry however, and was heaven-sent for his style of performance, had actually been developed between Alan Boyd and Bruce Forsyth during the show's early incarnations. Alan told Larry that Camera 3 would be trained on him at all times, ready for a close-up, so if he wanted to react, pull a face, or make an ad lib quip to the viewer at home, he could turn to Camera 3 at any time and know that the director would catch it. Larry's eyesight was so bad he couldn't see the numbers on the cameras unfortunately, so they had to put a big cardboard sign saying "LARRYCAM" over the top of Camera 3. His myopia aside, Larry instinctively understood the potential of interacting directly with the millions of viewers at home, and sharing something in confidence with them. This was a funny technique Larry used to great success, and indeed became a trademark of the show. He got some of his biggest laughs just with a withering look to Camera 3.

Larry still thought of himself as much more of a theatre performer than a broadcaster, so it suited him perfectly to record all *the Generation Games* in The BBC Television Theatre, which had previously been The Shepherd's Bush Empire, built in 1903 as a lavish music hall. Here he could feel as though he was playing to a theatre audience, and he could almost forget about all the television paraphernalia, which was pretty much irrelevant to him anyway.

When the news first leaked that Brucie's replacement was to be Larry people in the television industry had grave doubts that it could possibly work. TV critics sharpened their pencils, and their claws. Journalists circled like vultures around Larry, almost willing him to fail, constantly pointing out what a big responsibility he was taking on, and unkindly reminding him that Bruce Forsyth was a hard act to follow. Larry professed that he couldn't copy Bruce even if he wanted to, as he had only ever seen his version of the show once, that he could remember. This seems unlikely to be true, but it was a good way of stopping the subject of comparison in its tracks. He even told one showbiz columnist that he thought he might only be there for one series as Brucie would probably return once his ITV commitments had been fulfilled. Forsyth himself, very graciously, sent Larry a telegram wishing him luck with the show and saying: "Enjoy yourself... and do it your way".

The untransmitted pilot show was made, which, Bill Cotton admits in his autobiography, was a complete disaster. Larry was all over the place... But... it was funny...

Alan Boyd kept the faith however, instinctively knowing that Larry was right for the show and Isla was also right, even if a few minor adjustments had to be made about how the show was driven, and who would do the driving. In the current corporate, committee-driven world of television – 'focus groups' and statistical audience research panels would have probably used the pilot to spell the end for the new presenting team, but in those halcyon days a good producer's instinct was trusted and valued. Bill Cotton's highly experienced team knew they had the makings of a hit on their hands, even if Larry did have a few shortcomings as a game show host.

I know from having produced many TV game shows over the years myself that the much-maligned role of game show host is a very specialised and complex skill, and much harder than it looks. The performer has to be able to multi-task on many levels for a start. He or she has to be on top of the mechanics of the game at all times, acting as judge and referee, making sure all the rules are adhered to, and that the game play is progressing correctly and at the right pace, whilst remembering to stay calm and in control, and ideally being funny, avuncular, informative, witty, tough but sympathetic, and charming, all at the same time. They also have to be able to ad lib their way out of any situation, so their brain has to be in gear, and their wits highly tuned, from beginning to end. It is no coincidence that all the best game show hosts have been highly intelligent people – Bruce Forsyth, Bob Monkhouse, Tom O'Connor and Chris Tarrant being among the cream of the British crop. Larry, whilst charismatic and funny, wasn't anywhere near as sharp as these guys. It came as quite a shock to him just how much was involved. Deep down the powers-that-be at the BBC must have known that these were skills that Larry was never going to acquire in a month of Sundays.

Alan Boyd, with great foresight, had already provided himself with the perfect solution – his new find, Isla St Clair. Alan had been leaning this way during rehearsals anyway, but after the pilot recording Isla was given more responsibility to police the game itself, and keep the show together, allowing Larry to relax and actually capitalise on his own ineptitude, doing what he was best at – bumbling around, teasing the participants and being hilarious. That way Isla was able to gently but firmly guide the contestants (and Larry!) through the game.

Director Marcus Plantin went so far as to describe Isla as Larry's 'rock' – the person he knew he could turn to when he became so wrapped up in the moment that he couldn't remember what was supposed to happen next – something which frequently happened. Marcus said this wasn't to decry what Larry brought to the show, but Isla allowed him to relax and do what he was good at. Marcus added that there was never any doubt however that Larry was the star of the show.

In those early formative days Alan Boyd realised that Larry had one advantage over his predecessor, because he was willing to have a go at playing the games himself. Forsyth was a perfectionist and wasn't prepared to attempt anything unless he could do it perfectly. Larry however wasn't afraid of making a fool of himself, knowing the audience would love him for his ineptitude, so he'd happily muck in and have a go – usually with disastrous, but hilarious consequences. Alan says this gave the show a whole new dimension and an extra layer of comedy. Certainly some of the most memorable moments, many of which are immortalised on YouTube, are the catastrophic attempts made by Larry and Isla to play odd musical instruments, or dance or march with military precision. Their obvious joy at fooling around and their genuine giggles are infectious.

Boyd said he had great admiration for Larry's instinctive way of spotting where there was fun to be had out of something within certain games. Although some of Larry's supposed incompetence and uselessness was perfectly genuine, nevertheless the seasoned performer knew exactly where the comedy was, and he never missed a trick.

The first proper show was recorded in front of a large audience in the now defunct BBC Television Theatre in Shepherd's Bush. Larry was nervous. He turned all the lights out in his dressing room and lay down for a rest, to get his head together. Like the old pro that he was Larry was buoyed by the sound of the audience arriving over the little Tannoy speaker in his dressing room. The crowd's excited murmuring got the adrenaline flowing. Then producer Alan Boyd came in and told Larry to just go out there and have fun. He said the words that any performer loves to hear: "There is a lot of love for you in that theatre. We're all on your side. Go out there and enjoy it..."

The nerves lingered for the first few minutes, but once the laughs started coming Larry relaxed and did indeed enjoy himself. Isla made sure the game worked and the right teams won the prizes, and the audience went wild, giving the new Generation Game host a standing ovation at the end of the recording. Afterwards everybody was slapping Larry on the back, congratulating him and telling him he'd nailed it. Alan Boyd and Bill Cotton brought champagne into his dressing room, and reassured him that it had been successful and it was going to work. There must have been a lot of very relieved people that night, not least Larry Grayson himself.

That first show was transmitted the following Saturday evening, but Larry couldn't bear to watch it. He felt quite sick with worry about the reaction, knowing it was still a major gamble taking over a hit show from a popular host. Larry told Fan he was going out for a walk. Anxiously he paced round the block, occasionally glancing in through the windows of ordinary houses, seeing that they were watching him on their TV sets. Nobody seemed to be switching off, and people even seemed to be laughing. He relaxed a little. When he knew the show was over he returned home to find the phone was white hot with calls from friends, colleagues and admirers telling him what a triumph it had been. At last he could relax. Perhaps his new BBC bosses were right and it was going to work.

In fact it worked better than anybody could have imagined. The new look *Generation Game* didn't just maintain the high viewing figures which Bruce had been getting, but Larry actually pulled in several million new viewers to the programme. At one point eighteen million people were regularly tuning in to see Larry and Isla giggling their way through silly game after game, and their viewing figures peaked at well over twenty million. The public loved Larry's vulnerability and his honest authenticity, and giggled along with him and Isla every week.

The pairing of Larry and Isla was so popular that in 1980 they were flown out to California together by the BBC to make that year's annual favourite holiday programme *Disney Time*. Of course Larry was in his element in California. Tony Hawes, *The Generation Game*'s programme associate, flew out with them and got them involved in a big Laurel & Hardy convention out there, as they were all big fans of Stan and Ollie. There they were thrilled to meet Lois Laurel, Stan's daughter. Love blossomed for Tony Hawes and he married Lois the following year. During this visit Larry met and befriended craggy-faced Hollywood actor, Jack Klugman, star of *Quincy* and the TV version of *The Odd Couple*. I can't help thinking there can't have been an odder couple than Larry Grayson and Jack Klugman.

Conceding his doubts were unfounded, BBC1 boss Bill Cotton was delighted with the overwhelming public reaction, also admitting in his memoirs that it didn't exactly break his heart that *Bruce Forsyth's Big Night* had turned out to be an unmitigated disaster for ITV. It was slammed by the critics, and viewers switched channels, preferring to watch Brucie's old BBC show, with its new inept but very funny camp host. The more the critics ripped Forsyth's show to shreds, the more they sang the praises of Larry's revised version of the show Bruce had left, *The Generation Game*.

Paul Vaughan says that Larry was not nearly as inept as he had us all believe. With a little more rehearsal he could have done all the dance moves and all the challenges reasonably well, but that would have rubbed the contestants' noses in it, which just wasn't Larry's style. When Paul first asked him why he allowed himself to look as though he had two left feet all the time, Larry said: "I know what I'm doing duck..." He believed that it was better for him to look clumsy and to bungle his way through everything, to put the families at their ease and to allow them to shine.

Also, if he could make a fool of himself, then they wouldn't mind doing the same.

The first series of *Larry Grayson's Generation Game*, as it had been re-branded, ran for fifteen weeks. Each recording took three days to prepare, rehearse and record, but Larry hated staying in London, so he had his driver take him to a gay friend's hotel, 'The Jolly Sailor' in Thame in Oxfordshire for the middle two nights, where he would hold court in the private bar, gin and tonic in hand, entertaining the other residents. Then, after every single one of the recordings, he would get his chauffeur to drive the hundred or so miles back to Nuneaton, preferring to get home to Fan, rather than stay away from home another night.

Fastidious as ever, Larry's one indulgence was the purchase of a portable vacuum cleaner so that he could keep his BBC dressing room spotless. Isla St Clair said she was much less fussy and he'd come in with a reproachful look and vacuum her dressing room after she'd eaten a sandwich. Marcus Plantin said Isla almost treated Larry like an uncle or a father figure when they were off camera. He used to tick Isla off for eating too much. He once said: "You go on eating chocolate cake my girl and you may not put on weight yet, but you wait until you're older!" She'd just say: "Oh shut up Larry!" It was a very endearing relationship.

Alan Boyd told me that, unlike many performers, Larry enjoyed and reacted well to genuine surprises during the recordings. From very early on they had introduced sliding doors (which didn't always slide!) to reveal a surprise guest for Larry each week. Boyd says Larry really never did know who was going to come through those doors, and revelled in the revelation when it was somebody he liked and knew. Of course this had its own occasional snags. There were odd times when a guest celebrity would make a dramatic entrance through the doors into Larry's open arms, with Larry mouthing into the wings, over their shoulder: "No idea! Who is it?!" Isla would then be pushed hastily on to the studio floor to say to camera: "Will you please put your hands together for XXXX!".

The converse problem was if it was somebody he knew and loved Larry would forget the show and stand there gossiping away to them for ten minutes, which had to be heavily edited down to a more manageable length of chat before transmission. The show's director Marcus Plantin, who later became the producer of *The Generation Game* when Alan Boyd defected to London Weekend Television, fondly remembers a particularly magic moment when Larry's great friend Diana Dors walked out as the surprise guest from behind the sliding doors. Marcus said the whole television theatre audience erupted at the unexpected presence of this iconic superstar, and Larry was quite overcome to see her.

Larry's casual attitude towards the discipline of the show was what made him so relaxed and 'at home', but again it had its downside. After a few weeks a small, predominantly camp entourage had started to accompany Larry to The Television Theatre and would congregate in his dressing room before every *Generation Game* recording, naturally enough including Larry's 'personal assistant' Peter Smith. Of course they had nothing to do but enjoy themselves, whereas Larry had a show to do. Alan Boyd had to put his foot down in the end, especially when he saw that the hangers-on were plying Larry with gin and tonic before a show. Bill Cotton had a strict rule that his performers were not allowed alcohol before a recording, and Boyd wanted his new star to focus on the job in hand, and to keep a clear head, so he had to be firm with the entourage. Larry could be quite obstinate when told what he could and couldn't do, and he demanded to have a small gin and tonic to calm his nerves before a show. Boyd shrewdly made sure that a gin bottle was supplied to his dressing room full of flat tonic water, so that what Larry actually drank to calm his nerves before a recording was in fact tonic and tonic. Larry's driver had learned a clever addition to this useful trick – he'd rub a little gin around the rim of the glass, so that Larry could smell it, which made the fake tipple even more convincing.

In those days at the BBC there was continuity of crewing and support staff, so the whole regular team became almost like a family, according to Marcus Plantin. He said everybody enjoyed working with Larry, and the whole experience of those four years was never anything but joyous.

Isla St Clair has said on numerous occasions that Larry felt *The Generation Game* was the pinnacle of his career, and he loved it, being old and mature enough to enjoy the adulation without it going to his head. She said that whilst he was always the consummate professional, and his many years of experience was utilised at all times, it was endearing that he was genuinely touched by his fame, and very grateful for it, having struggled for so long to get there. He himself said it was the happiest show of his life. Isla believes that every contestant went away happy, feeling that Larry had spent quality time with them. He always had time for people, because he truly adored his public.

The only sad thing that Isla St Clair has said is that Larry couldn't bring himself to watch tapes of the old shows after his time on *The Generation Game* finished, because the show had been so important to him, and such fun, that he would have found it a painful reminder of what he was missing to see them again. He must have known that he would never recapture those dizzy heights, which of course he never did.

I asked Alan Boyd if he enjoyed working with Larry. He said it was always easy and relaxed, but very different from working with Bruce Forsyth, the perfectionist, who always needed to rehearse, rehearse again, analyse, and work out every last detail. Bruce would almost drive the content of the show himself, fussing over things and being quite demanding, whereas Larry would just come in and see what the production team had put together, allowing the show they had created to drive his performance. In crude terms I suppose you could say that the early *Generation Games* happened because of Bruce and the way he was, whereas the later shows happened around Larry, almost despite him. Both ways it has to be said worked brilliantly.

Larry did need constant reassurance as a performer however, which made him quite high maintenance. *The Generation Game* was a totally free-wheeling show, with very little script, relying heavily on Larry's ability to ad lib and have fun with the contestants, so it was even more important for somebody to be there at all times to pander to the star of the show's ego and to boost his confidence. Larry's maverick manager Peter Dulay was beginning to fall out of favour, so was never around for very long at recordings of *The Generation Game*, if at all. Larry's friend Paul Vaughan filled the breech and attended every single recording, waiting in the wings to reassure Larry that he had been hilarious, and reminding him of the highlights of that particular show. Paul told me it wasn't difficult to do so, as it really was so funny, and there really were lots of highlights to recount. By the fourth year of Larry's tenure Paul Vaughan had become Larry's personal manager, and a very attentive manager it has to be said. Paul was very experienced and well-suited to the role, having looked after a raft of major stars, including Chris Tarrant.

There is no doubt that Peter Dulay had been good for Larry, and had been the one who finally paved the way for the stardom that had eluded Larry for so many years. Larry owed Dulay a lot. The trouble was that Dulay was perhaps taking a little more than he was owed. Larry was naïve and disinterested when it came to business matters. That's what he paid his support team for – to look after all those boring details. There was always plenty of money available when he wanted something, and there was definitely more money around than he and Fan had ever been used to having, so he didn't bother to check whether the sums added up properly. It took his bank to question his finances. They reasoned that with Larry at the top, working so hard and so frequently, and doing so many lucrative television programmes for the BBC, there wasn't as much flowing into his account as they would have expected.

Larry's entourage of hangers-on and camp followers even started questioning Larry's income, realising that there was something drastically wrong. Dulay had Larry making personal appearances, and opening supermarkets up and down the country for extremely large cash sums. A lot of this money was spirited away to a Spanish bank account, as an investment for the future, but Larry never saw so much as a penny of it. Peter Dulay had been a scriptwriter, so, on top of his substantial management fees, and considerable expenses, he was also charging Larry sizeable fees for writing jokes, which Larry rarely saw, and never used. Even the BBC payments for *The Generation Game* seemed to be far lower than the contract stated, by the time they actually reached Larry's local bank.

Former BBC executive and long time friend of Larry's, Kevin Bishop, said he had heard that there were question marks over Dulay's handling of Larry's finances, but was shocked and surprised at the time. Kevin says Dulay was a genuinely nice guy, who had always been straightforward in his business dealings with him. Handling somebody else's money however carries great temptations.

Friends and colleagues thought Larry should have the unpleasant matter investigated properly and that he should take legal action. He completely refused, not wanting the negative press that a court case would attract, and quite simply not wanting any distasteful aggravation. As I have said before Larry hated confrontation. He also reasoned that he was universally perceived, for good reason, as one of the nice guys of showbusiness, so he didn't want that image tarnished by the kind of mud-slinging that would inevitably have ensued if he had aggressively pursued the matter through the courts. He figured the best damage limitation would be to write off his considerable financial losses, sever ties with Peter Dulay, and quietly regroup for a brighter future with his new manager Paul Vaughan, who was a very shrewd businessman, and a good friend in whom Larry could trust implicitly.

There was a predicament however, as the problems hadn't officially been aired. The way the BBC contracts department works is that if an agent has negotiated on behalf of a client for the first series of a television programme, they will only deal with that same agent for any subsequent series. This is to stop unscrupulous performers getting an agent to do the dirty work for the initial contract, then cutting them out of their entitled commission ever afterwards. In Larry's case this meant that the BBC would still only deal with Peter Dulay when it came to any contracts for *The Generation Game.* Larry found this situation intolerable, but unavoidable, unless he went public with his reasons for the split with Dulay.

Paul Vaughan says there were actually two reasons that Larry walked away from *The Generation Game*, after four record-breaking years. The first reason was the fact that he didn't want Peter Dulay earning any more commission from him. The other reason was that he rightly felt the show was becoming repetitive and had run out of new ideas. He was reassured by showbiz friends, notably Penelope Keith, who told him that it was always wise to quit a show while it's still on top, rather than have the embarrassment of everybody seeing it looking jaded, its popularity dwindling, and its success just fading away. It was a hard decision to make, but Larry honourably went to inform his BBC bosses, so that they were the first to know of his intentions to quit, expecting them to understand, and presuming that they would just offer him a new show to make instead, as he'd done so well for them in recent years. He couldn't have been more wrong. The BBC never like their stars calling the shots and in fact they were angry at Larry walking out on such a big hit show. They saw it as a betrayal. Not only did they refuse to find him anything else to do, but they tried to spin the story to the press that the show had been axed, and Larry had been dropped.

Apparently Jimmy Tarbuck was approached by the BBC to take over *The Generation Game*, but Tarbie was too smart to try to follow the two maestros that had made the show such a big hit. The only way was down for the next host. The show didn't in fact return to our screens again until Bruce Forsyth returned to breathe fresh air back into the format in 1990, with a new co-host, Rosemarie Ford.

14

... Torquay beckons... and reluctant semi-retirement...

Peter Dulay quietly disappeared to Spain where he could retire very comfortably, leaving Paul Vaughan to worry about what was going to happen to Larry Grayson's career. The truth was Dulay had already had the best years. Things weren't so bad at first. Larry, fresh from his massive success on *The Generation Game*, was still hugely popular with the public, so he could command top money making personal appearances, and doing successful pantomimes and summer seasons, but he was nearly sixty and not wanting to kill himself working twice nightly for the rest of his life. There were of course odd television appearances – he'd always had a real affection and affinity for *The Good Old Days*, the BBC old time music hall variety show, so he appeared on that a few times, as well as becoming a semi-regular on Terry Wogan's *Blankety-Blank*. With his love of talking he did all the chat shows of the time, however no television company was offering him a series.

In 1983, to celebrate Larry's sixtieth birthday, London Weekend Television made a tribute programme, which was part documentary, part studio celebration, called *At Home with Larry Grayson*. Janet Street-Porter took Larry back to the Nuneaton of his childhood, including Abbey Green Infants School for a nostalgic dance around the maypole. They also popped in to The Fife Street Working Men's Club, the place where Larry made his first professional appearance, for a reunion with Freda Freeman and a gang of old friends. He couldn't resist the urge to sing his signature song from those days, "In the Bushes at the Bottom of the Garden". It was then on to

Christow village hall in Devon where he began his tour with Harry Leslie in *Tomorrow's Stars*. There were even glimpses into his home in Nuneaton, with Fan making a rare appearance in front of the camera, and there were shots of his retreat in Torquay. In the studio Larry chatted about his life, and Janet reunited him with close friends like Arthur Marshall, John Hanson and of course Noele Gordon. It was a very happy programme, but it was much more like a tribute to somebody looking back on a life and career that is virtually over, than the launch of a new chapter.

During these autumn years of his life Larry got to hear about a local council committee meeting where it was proposed that Nuneaton should have a Close in a new housing estate named after Larry Grayson, in honour of their most famous son. Small town mentality and even smaller-minded prejudices still abounded however, and one councillor stood up and vetoed the idea, saying that he didn't think it was appropriate for the town to be associated with somebody 'of his type'. Larry was understandably incensed by this homophobic snub. He quite rightly believed that he had done more than most to put Nuneaton on the map. On hearing about the council's decision not to honour him Larry left strict instructions with friends and family that no memorial was ever to be erected in Nuneaton, posthumously or otherwise. If the civic pen-pushers were ashamed of him now, then they weren't going to bask in the glory of his fame and success in years to come. He also made the drastic decision to leave the area all together, and turn his back on the town which he had been proud to call home for so many years, but had now so ungraciously rebuffed him. In 1983, with nothing special to look forward to careerwise, Larry decided, perhaps hastily, to sell up in Nuneaton and retire with Fan and his poodle 'Arthur Marshall' to his favourite bolthole Torquay, or Britain's Beverly Hills as he called it.

The official story for the press was that he was retiring from the business to live by the sea and take life easy. He told journalists he didn't want to end up like Tommy Cooper and Eric Morecambe who had died on stage, because they had overdone things and worked too hard.

When the news broke that Larry was leaving Nuneaton a local journalist called Steve Read wrote a piece in The Nuneaton Tribune with the headline "Larry: Did we let him down?". Steve reminded Nuneatonians that Larry had remained loyal to their hometown all his life and had proudly mentioned his Midlands roots at every opportunity. He queried why Larry had not even been invited by the council to switch on the town's new Christmas lights, and questioned whether the people of Nuneaton had taken their most famous son for granted. Steve said the town should have honoured Larry in the same way that Rochdale honoured their most famous inhabitant, Gracie Fields. It was too little too late – Larry had already made up his mind.

By the end of 1983 'The Garlands', his detached Nuneaton home throughout all the successful years, was sold, along with his small Torquay apartment, and a beautifully elegant house, set in its own extensive grounds overlooking the sea, was found in an exclusive area of Torquay called The Lincombes, not far from his old apartment in Thatcher Avenue. Larry bought the well-appointed luxury house from a famous footballer who was 'down-sizing'. Number 2 Haldon Close, his new magnificent five-bedroom, two-bathroom home, seemed like everything he'd worked for. He had never been extravagant, and Paul Vaughan had helped him make some wise investments, so Larry wasn't short of money. He could easily have afforded a housekeeper, but he preferred to don an apron and do all the vacuuming, cleaning and washing-up himself, while Fan did all the cooking. They had once tried employing a cleaning lady when they were living in Nuneaton, but Larry was so fussy about household chores that the minute she'd gone he went right round the house, following in her footsteps, cleaning everything again. He was still not keen on getting his hands dirty however, so his one extravagant indulgence was a gardener to tend the grounds.

Larry thought this would be the perfect way to spend his twilight years, living in luxury by the sea, surrounded by close friends, and looking back fondly on an extraordinary life. Unfortunately this wasn't quite how it worked out, and it is where his love affair with Torquay started to turn sour. At first he was happy enjoying the sea air and pottering off to do a bit of shopping with Fan in the upmarket Wellswood area, or have tea and cakes with friends at Madge Mellor's café in nearby Newton Abbott. As late as the end of 1984, in one of his many letters to his dedicated fan and pen friend Pauline Pearson, Larry tells her that he is still loving living in the Torquay area. However, with the Grayson name no longer quite so much in the spotlight, or the headlines, the circle of sycophantic friends and the entourage of camp followers had gradually started to disappear. Beautiful as Devon undoubtedly is, it is pretty cut off, and genuine friends from further afield found a visit quite a trek, so visitors were few and far between. His dear friend and neighbour Gwen Berryman had died in late 1983, and poor Fan was beginning to fail.

Remember Fan was fourteen years older than Larry, so she was seventy-five by the time they made the big move to the south coast. Her short term memory wasn't what it had been, and she was beginning to show early signs of dementia. In the big house Fan had an annexed wing all to herself. Much to Larry's fond amusement Fan, renowned for her malapropisms, always referred to the annexe as 'the anorak'. They were a little way out of the centre of Torquay in a 'much sought after' select area, but it was very sedate and quiet, vastly different from Nuneaton where friends and neighbours were constantly popping in. There was a Rolls Royce and a Saab in the garage, but Larry couldn't drive them, so he and Fan were quite isolated from the life and fun of Torbay. Larry had found a local taxi driver who would drop everything and act as his chauffeur when needed, but of course you don't book a chauffeur just to pop into town for a bit of shopping. Larry, for the first time in his life, was bored. He was missing showbusiness... and beginning to feel lonely and unloved...

To relieve the boredom, with time on his hands for the first time in years, Larry took off on a pilgrimage to his beloved Hollywood, in an homage to all the wonderful stars he'd worshipped for so long from afar. In another letter to Pauline Pearson, in September 1985, he tells her that he's had a bad year healthwise, so he is treating himself to this exciting sojourn to Los Angeles in October. One of the highlights of the trip was putting his own hands into the impressions made by the hands of his screen idols in the concrete outside the legendary Chinese Theatre on The Hollywood Walk Of Fame. He did all the touristy things and looked at all the famous studios, and the Beverly Hills homes of the stars, but what he'd really loved so much about Hollywood was long gone. The visit was a success though, and he loved to tell people about this magical trip of a lifetime.

Larry and Fan did stay in Torquay for a couple of years, at the end of which Fan was needing a lot of care and attention and couldn't really be left. A care home was soon going to be the only real solution. Larry began to beat himself up about Fan, who had been terribly lonely and a fish out of water in Torquay. She'd sit in her annexe just staring at the walls, not going out, and rarely seeing anybody but Larry from one week to the next. He believed, rightly or wrongly, that the move to Torquay, and her subsequent boredom and loneliness, had hastened the onset of Fan's senility. He never did forgive himself for imposing that drastic lifestyle change upon her, even though she would almost certainly have succumbed to dementia just the same if they'd remained in Nuneaton.

One dark and gloomy winter's afternoon Larry phoned Paul Vaughan and said that all he'd done all day was sit staring out of the window. The sea was so grey, and the sky was so grey that he could barely tell where one ended and the other started. Larry said the only excitement had been a darker grey cargo ship which had slowly passed along the horizon. He said he'd watched it for over an hour before it finally disappeared from view. His concluding words to Paul were desperate and unusually strong: "Get me out of this fucking place!".

Fortunately the Torquay mansion had appreciated in value, and it sold quite quickly for a considerable profit. Larry was so relieved when he finally turned his back on Torquay. He swallowed his pride for Fan's sake, and returned home to Nuneaton, where he and Fan moved into a brand new development of bungalows which had just been built, called Harcourt Gardens, which was within easy reach of the town centre. The money from the sale of the big house and grounds in Torquay was more than sufficient to buy two of these small bungalows, at much cheaper Midlands prices. Larry lived in number 4 Harcourt Gardens, which he called 'Cascade', and he put Fan in the adjoining bungalow.

In 1986 a lifeline was thrown to Larry by Anglia Television. They wanted him to host a game show called *Sweethearts* for ITV. His first reaction was to say no, but he was eventually talked into it. Perhaps it would have been better if he had stood by his first instincts. A series of twelve shows was made in November 1986, which aired in the spring of 1987. The idea was for a panel of three celebrities to spend half an hour guessing which of three couples were real life sweethearts, telling the true story of how they met. The other two couples were unknown actors reciting stories of true love meetings sent in by viewers.

The shows all started with the famous Anglia Television announcer John Benson saying things like: "Cupid took flight at Luton! ... What this lady learned from her driving lessons! ... And a chauvinist pig in a pickle! ... But which is the real romance? ... Cross his heart, not even he knows... so open that door for *Sweethearts* sleuth Larry Grayson!"

Sweethearts was hailed as Larry's big television comeback, with a press publicity campaign branding him as 'the sweetheart sleuth'.

However the format was ultimately lacklustre and ITV rather buried the series by scheduling it up against BBC1's ratings juggernaut *EastEnders*, so consequently *Sweethearts* flopped and wasn't recommissioned. Larry hadn't particularly liked the fact that it was all recorded in Norwich, so far from home and Fan. He also felt that Norwich, being so remote, wasn't the best place to attract the right celebrity panellists, or the best couples as contestants. *Sweethearts* was quietly forgotten by both ITV and Larry Grayson.

Fan had become a major concern, even though Larry still wanted to carry on performing. He turned down several offers of theatre work, but was grateful for an offer of pantomime over the Christmas and New Year period (1987 / 1988) at The Alexandra Theatre in Birmingham, alongside TV's 'Supergran' Gudrun Ure and local star Les Ross. The panto was not one he was normally associated with, *Dick Whittington*, and he found doing the show twice nightly an exhausting experience, but the attraction to Larry was that it was close to home, which meant he could get back every night to check on Fan. He endearingly said at the time: "It's the least I can do after she brought me up like she did."

15

... a question of entertainment...

In 1987 my own life coincided with Larry's for the first time, and began a period of around nine months where I had the privilege of working with him, and getting to know him reasonably well. Like most people in that fortunate position I found that I liked him very much, and even better he always made me laugh... a lot. God bless anybody that makes me laugh. I, like most people in Britain, was totally oblivious to the trials and tribulations of his life at that time. I was just a fan. I'd never met him, or even seen him perform live on stage, but I'd always found his TV appearances joyously funny and endearing. I perceived him as one of the giants of the industry at that time. I don't think I was even aware of *Sweethearts*, and I certainly don't ever recall seeing it, however I had watched and enjoyed Larry right from his earliest appearances on *Saturday Variety*, right through his own shows and all *The Generation Game* years. I also always tried to catch him on any television guest appearance doing a bit of the act, or on a chat show, where he always excelled, being a man who was never short of something funny to say.

At the time I was working for the BBC at New Broadcasting House in Manchester, making networked BBC1 and BBC2 programmes for the then thriving entertainment department. I had only been working in television production for around four years, but I was rising nicely through the system and I was an Assistant Producer, on the cusp of becoming a Producer, which I did become just a few months later. I was working most of the time with an Executive Producer called Alan Walsh, who had taken me under his wing and had mentored me in the ways of the BBC. He'd also taught me a lot about the inner workings of television production. Not only that but we had become great friends. Alan's team, which included me as his Assistant Producer, had just completed the making of *The Grand Knockout Tournament* at Alton Towers – the spectacular all-star Royal Family edition of *It's A Knockout*. It had been a uniquely bizarre, exciting, funny and incredibly surreal experience, but that is a story for another time... and possibly another book.

BBC Manchester was the home of *A Question of Sport*. Probably still is. Alan Walsh had the ingenious idea of borrowing the brand to make a showbiz quiz with teams of stars answering questions on showbusiness: *A Question of Entertainment*. It was a simple enough notion, but I thought it was a great idea. On the strength of our record-breaking viewing figures for the 'Royal Knockout' he had been given the go-ahead to make a pilot of this new fun quiz / celebrity panel game. The first thing he did was call a meeting of his key team members to discuss the format and how we should progress. He had asked us to come along with suggestions for the casting of the chairman and the two regular team captains. They all three obviously had to be old hands with a wealth of knowledge and experience in the world of entertainment in all its many forms. They also had to be funny. I had gone along with my dream team, which I put forward at the meeting: Tom O'Connor in the chair, umpiring the sparring between two elder statesmen of comedy, team captains Ken Dodd and Larry Grayson. Alan liked all three ideas, but thought I was maybe being a little over-ambitious as they were all major players at that time, and he felt that such big stars might not want to share equal billing. Nevertheless, as with all casting, it is better to start off setting your sights high, as they can always be lowered if you get a few 'no thank yous', so Alan told me to contact their agents and take all three stars out to lunch to try to persuade them to do the show.

I was very excited about the prospect of having lunch with these three icons of the comedy game, all of whom I found very funny men. Like Larry himself I have never quite got used to meeting up with my heroes and idols on an equal footing, and it is always a thrill. Lunch with Ken Dodd was agreeable, but very business-like. There were no jokes at all, which seemed strange from arguably the most prolific gagsmith of all time, but we got on well and, more importantly, he seemed keen on the idea of the show. Next was Tom O'Connor, who was one of the nicest people you could hope to meet – charming, gentle, intelligent, witty, funny, and with that agreeable knack of making you feel important. He always gave the impression that he was genuinely pleased to see you, and share his latest hilarious anecdote, or bit of showbiz gossip. Tom also liked the idea of the show. So far it looked as though I'd got two out of two of my dream team signed up, subject to contract negotiations. Finally I travelled to Birmingham to have lunch with Larry Grayson, who brought his manager Paul Vaughan along for moral support. I had actually known Paul for quite a number of years through my close association with his other major client, Chris Tarrant, which I thought might make the meeting easier. I needn't have worried. I took to Larry straight away, and fortunately he seemed to take to me.

I have already said at the beginning of this book that it was, and still is, the most hilarious lunch I have ever had in my entire life. However, if you interrogated and tortured me for a month I couldn't tell you one single funny thing that Larry said that day – it was just a stream of side-splitting nonsense, gossip, and whimsy, just like his act. All I know is that the three of us laughed ourselves silly until we were politely but firmly thrown out of the hotel dining room, after five joyous hours, so that they could re-set the tables for dinner. That was one of the many times in my career when I couldn't believe I was actually being paid to have such a good time. I have been very fortunate. Oh, and somewhere in amongst all the hilarity we did discuss the programme, which Larry liked the sound of, and I had the third member of my dream team signed up. My executive producer Alan Walsh was very pleased with me. I must admit I was rather pleased with myself, as this programme with these three giants of the world of comedy was going to be a joy to make, which indeed it proved to be.

Unfortunately, because the lunch with Larry had been such a hoot for all concerned, perhaps our attention was not as focussed as it should have been. There was one misunderstanding, which didn't come to light right away. Paul Vaughan still claims that I misled them. In fact the innocent misunderstanding was on both sides, and neither side was trying to mislead the other. Our showbiz quiz was going to focus mainly on film and television questions, plus, to a lesser extent, popular music, stage and radio. It was a massive bonus therefore, or so I thought, when Paul told me over lunch that Larry's knowledge of cinema was encyclopaedic. I hadn't known that about him, and I thought it would add a real extra dimension every time one of our team captains astounded us with his endless outpourings about any movie we could mention. What he didn't tell me was that Larry's interest in, and knowledge of, cinema ended around the mid 1950s. I assumed he'd be equally conversant with James Bond, *Star Wars*, *Carry On*, Dustin Hoffman, Raquel Welch and Jane Fonda as he was with *Brief Encounter*, *Casablanca*, *The Wizard of Oz*, Clark Gable and Myrna Loy. Of course I couldn't have been more wrong. He'd stopped going to the cinema all together by the 1960s. Paul says that he and Larry went away with the impression that we were making a quiz that was going to be all about vintage and classic cinema, which would give Larry a chance to show off his massive knowledge of The Golden Age of Hollywood. In fact the BBC wanted a celebrity quiz that was fun to play at home, with contemporary questions about modern popular culture. Fortunately the misunderstanding didn't seem to matter. Larry threw himself into the game with gusto, and appeared to enjoy himself... and was very competitive!

Another gratifying side effect of my casting choices was that Larry became great friends with Ken Dodd. I don't think that they'd ever met before, but they became friendly rivals within the game, and mutual admirers off-screen. They loved swapping hilarious showbiz anecdotes in our Green Room after every recording, clearly enjoying each other's company, and making us all laugh in the process. It was a rare privilege to be there. In fact Ken paid a very touching tribute to Larry after his death, and appeared in a couple of retrospective documentaries about Larry's life. It's pleasing to think that they met because of me.

Booking guests for any pilot show is always tricky, as pilots are rarely transmitted, so the guests have very little to gain from being there, unlike the regulars who are hoping to be contracted to make a whole lucrative, high profile series. This was especially true with *A Question of Entertainment*. All I had to offer guests was a small fee, knowing that they'd have to travel to Manchester to do the show. Isla St Clair hadn't really had much TV work since *The Generation Game*, so she was readily available, and I thought it would put Larry at his ease having somebody he knew so well sitting beside him on his team, so I signed her up. In fact Larry was surprisingly grumpy about it and demanded to know why I'd booked her, saying waspishly: "She won't know anything!". My heart was in the right place, and the audience seemed pleased to see them reunited, even if Larry wasn't quite so thrilled.

The pilot show went well, and we were commissioned to make a meaty series of eighteen thirty-minute programmes for a highly prestigious family viewing slot: 7.15pm every Sunday evening on BBC1. The only comment from the powers-that-be was to make sure it stayed modern, cutting edge and contemporary. This was becoming a mantra with television executives at that time. They were already getting jittery about 'old school' comedians, and were beginning to turn their backs on previously iconic entertainers. Alternative comedy was the new up-and-coming thing, but I always felt that the BBC should have catered for all tastes, with all kinds of comedy entertainment. That lamentable period where numerous hugely popular 'babies' were thrown out with the mainstream 'bath water' is thankfully over, and the BBC schedulers seem happy to have the mainstream talents of Peter Kay, Lee Mack and Michael McIntyre, comfortably sitting alongside the more cutting edge, harder-hitting comedy of shows like *Mock the Week*.

I virtually produced *A Question of Entertainment*, casting and booking all the guest team panellists, writing most of the questions, and briefing all three of the stars, and their guest team members, on every aspect of the show. Because I'd set the questions, and went through them all with Tom O'Connor before every recording, he liked me to sit near the front in the studio audience, in his direct eye-line, so that he could turn to me as an official adjudicator for a thumbs-up or a thumbs-down if there were ever any ambiguous answers, or if any team member came up with a partial answer or a plausible sounding alternative. Larry and I were getting on so well he capitalised on me sitting in the front of the audience as well, but, in his case, for more comedic purposes. Basically he relentlessly made fun of me and used me as the butt of many jokes, week in, week out. He'd point me out and say, with disdain: "Ooh look at 'im sitting there! They do let some riff-raff in here!" ... "What's the matter with 'im?! Common as dirt! Don't stare!" When ever there was an "im" – it was me... Or he'd come out with some piece of mildly salacious and very funny gossip, then turn to where I was sitting and say: "I told you in bed this morning, didn't I?" ... Then, with a toss of his head and pursed lips, he'd look away and hilariously add: "He's a liar – I never mentioned it...". Far from being offended or embarrassed by his jibes, I loved every minute of it.

Larry continued to make me laugh, and we were getting on very well, but it soon started to become obvious that he was developing a bit of a crush on me, which had to remain an unrequited crush as I am not gay. It was never a problem, but when he'd had a gin and tonic in the Green Room after a show he did start to become a little more amorous and was all over me. He came up with the funniest chat-up line I have ever heard in my entire life: "Oh Tony – let's run away to Torquay together and open a little wool shop". I laughed and reminded him that I was a happily married man with a toddler son and a wife at home. He wasn't to be deterred by such a trivial detail: "Tell me where she lives" he said with an impish twinkle, "I'll put a bomb through the letterbox and blow her up!". That was all light-hearted hilarious banter obviously, but I thought it maybe hid a sad truth.

I certainly didn't mind his attention, but I felt a bit sorry for him that he was wasting his time with me, and I worried he was possibly lonely and unfulfilled. I think I was probably right. Looking back I do think it was probably a bit of a 'thing' with him to try it on with a sympathetic straight guy, who wouldn't take offence or get angry. I think he knew it couldn't possibly go anywhere, but he probably got a kick out of the flirting. He may have even been relieved that no physical demands were going to be made of him, as he did always profess a revulsion of any form of physical sex act, or "pushing and shoving" as he called it.

Although Larry's advances and the odd clumsy lunge never felt awkward in any way, Paul Vaughan did intervene and, from then on, kept Larry well away from me once he'd had a drink. Larry couldn't handle alcohol terribly well. The old expression "one drink and he's anybody's" springs to mind, for obvious reasons. It only took one gin for him to start getting a bit giddy and also a bit frisky. When he was sober he behaved impeccably and we had a very good working relationship, and I'd also like to think a mutually happy friendship.

The 'try-ons' didn't appear to be a monotonously regular thing with him. There were lots of other young men around, and I was never aware of him making any other advances. As I have mentioned previously the only other similar instance I witnessed, after Paul Vaughan's ban on him being with me in the Green Room, was Larry, gin and tonic in hand of course, pinning Tony Blackburn into a corner. Poor Tony looked petrified.

The series was a complete labour of love for me, and we had some terrific guests come on when they heard who their team captains were going to be, and what a great slot we had been given by BBC1 on Sunday evenings. Stars like Thora Hird, Lionel Jeffries, Simon Dee, Roy Castle, Andrew Sachs, Bernard Bresslaw, Alfred Marks, Roy Kinnear and Brian Blessed all spring to mind as real treats to have around, plus lots of the major stars of the big shows of that period, as well as all the top mainstream comedians of the 1980s.

Most of the time it was all fun and laughter making the shows, but there are two stories that are probably worth recounting, as they maybe reveal a couple of insights into the Larry Grayson psyche.

The first one was a casting problem. I had booked Wincey Willis for one show to be on Larry's team. I admit she was not the greatest booking of all time, but she was popular in that period as the chirpy *Good Morning Britain* weather girl on breakfast television at TV-am, and she was also famous for appearing with Anneka Rice and Kenneth Kendall on Channel 4's big hit game show *Treasure Hunt*. When Larry arrived at the studio and found out that she was on his team that day he went ballistic and sent Paul Vaughan to inform us that Larry would not be appearing with Ms Willis, and we had no business booking her in the first place. I argued that I couldn't possibly have known of this unexpected personality clash, and Wincey certainly hadn't mentioned anything when I booked her and briefed her on the show. (I assume she was completely oblivious to the reason Larry had taken against her.) We'd never previously had any casting problems, and we'd never been given a 'black list' by either team captain of people they refused to work with.

It all got very heated, and, for once, I was glad I didn't have the actual title of producer, so it fell to Alan Walsh to solve the thorny problem. It got to the point where Paul informed us that Larry would not appear on the set if Wincey was not dismissed and sent home. Alan bravely called Larry's bluff and said she could not be de-booked, but if Larry really felt so strongly about it then he could go home and we could substitute comedian Stu Francis as Ken Dodd's opposing team captain for that particular show, as Stu happened to still be in the building, having just completed recording another show. After a brief stand-off, with neither side giving an inch, an uneasy compromise was reached. An expedient team reshuffle was quickly undertaken so that Wincey was now on Ken's team, and Larry grudgingly did the show. Obviously he wasn't going to let his team captain's chair be filled by Stu Francis, even for just one show. I never did discover what Wincey Willis did to earn Larry's ire, because he always seemed to get on so well with everybody, so she'd obviously done something that he considered to be terrible. It is a mystery up there with 'The Marie Celeste' and The Bermuda Triangle.

The other problem was with a particular film clip we used in one show. I have to admit I didn't like it either, but Alan Walsh had acquired a trailer for a brand new Barry Humphries film, *Les Patterson Saves The World*, which he wanted to feature in our quiz. It was for a "What happens next?" round. The film was a gross-out lavatorial comedy with crude and vulgar jokes, which I think bombed at the box office, and was quietly forgotten about by all concerned, especially Barry Humphries. Alan thought it would be amusing to use a clip where notoriously flatulent Sir Les Patterson, 'Cultural Attaché to Australia', played by Humphries, turns his back on a naked flame and an Arab ambassador at a United Nations meeting. We froze the film as Sir Les bent over, and poor Tom O'Connor had to ask: "What happens next?" It was pretty darned obvious what was going to happen next to be honest, so neither team would articulate their prediction, as they were all, to their credit, above stating the crude obvious. What happened next of course was that Sir Les Patterson broke wind with such alarming ferocity that the naked flame ignited his jet of human gas and cremated the Arab ambassador – which I've just realised actually sounds far funnier in print than it was when played out in graphic detail on screen.

When the denouement of the clip was shown to the studio audience Larry hit the roof. He hated it. I have to say, on this occasion I was on his side, but I was surprised by the extent of his extreme displeasure and outrage. Again Paul Vaughan was sent to see Alan Walsh after the recording, with dark threats about what would happen if that section wasn't edited out of the show. I think Alan conceded he had made a serious error of judgment, but it would have been a very difficult edit to remove the offending clip and its accompanying question, not least the fact that there was nothing to replace it with, and the programme would have run short, with an inexplicably uncomfortable jump to another round of the game.

As it happens fate had taken a hand, which mercifully got us all off the hook. It wasn't a happy quirk of fate, but it did perversely solve the problem in such a way that allowed everybody's dignity and pride to remain intact, and we could all get on with making the series without any further ill feeling. It was a rather sad reason though that ironically helped us out of this awkward hole.

It so happened that on that particular show I had booked crooner and 1950s heartthrob Frankie Vaughan to be a team member. Alarm bells had rung to be honest when I phoned him a few days before the show. His onstage persona was to be super-cool and laidback, but it struck me he was taking laidback to ridiculous extremes. It was hard work to get much out of him at all. The truth was, putting it diplomatically, that he seemed to be not as 'on the ball' as perhaps he had been in his younger days. When it came to the recording he couldn't answer a single question, not even a very simple one which I'd specifically created for him about a highlight of his own career – making a film in Hollywood. His answer was supposed to spark an amusing anecdote about working with Marilyn Monroe, which I'd eventually coaxed out of him over the phone. Not only did he fail to answer the easy question correctly, but he forgot his anecdote as well.

To his eternal credit Tom O'Connor generously did his best to prompt him to tell the promised story, saying helpfully: "So Frankie I understand you actually made a movie with Marilyn Monroe..." Frankie just nodded and agreed that he had. Tom apologised to me afterwards for not eliciting the story I'd hoped for, but he'd done everything he possibly could to give Frankie his moment of glory. Frankie then just sat looking slightly bemused and grinning, not answering another question or saying much throughout the entire recording. It was actually toe-curlingly embarrassing. What with that and the debacle with Larry over the smutty film clip I think we were all relieved when that day was over to be honest, which was unusual on such a happy show.

The decision was made to save Frankie's blushes and not transmit that show, consigning the video tape to the BBC vaults, unseen. Of course the upside of that difficult decision was that it solved the problem of the offending Barry Humphries clip at a stroke. The show and everything in it was like it had never been recorded. It was an expensive solution, as a whole new show had to be cast, created and recorded to replace the untransmitted episode, but it did completely airbrush away two serious dilemmas. Larry's moral compass could remain unsullied, and seasoned old showbiz pro Frankie Vaughan was not robbed of his ageing dignity in front of millions of viewers.

What was fascinating about both the Wincey Willis crisis and the Barry Humphries clip dilemma was the strength of feeling and the vehemence with which Larry fought his corner. Most of the time he was hilarious, happy-go-lucky, carefree Larry Grayson, but then these towering rages would emerge from nowhere. They seemed disproportionate to the problem to be honest, unless Wincey Willis had once strangled, cooked and eaten one of his beloved poodles of course.

Interestingly Larry said in an interview around that time: "I have a temper. I get angry, but it soon goes. If I'm upset everything falls around me, things seem bigger than they really are. I'm terribly sorry when I've shouted and raved, but I've got to have my say. It worries me though if I make anybody unhappy."

The film clip I suppose proved that Larry really was the prude he had always professed to be. Some performers claim to be quite prudish, almost as a smokescreen for their own naughty excesses, but they aren't really prudish at all. Larry obviously did have very clear boundaries. Clear to him at any rate. The Barry Humphries clip was undoubtedly tacky, but, the way Larry reacted, you would have thought we'd shown the most depraved pornography ever produced to a conference of shy nuns. There were shaken heads and disapproving tuts from Ken Dodd and the other celebrities, but not the extreme reaction which Larry demonstrated. One could actually be forgiven for accusing him of hypocrisy when you think of some of the things he said in his act.

Of course we all have our own individual line drawn in the sand, regarding personal censorship and what is morally acceptable and what isn't. I feel sure that some people might find incendiary flatulence marginally less offensive than a risqué line which Larry used often, even on television: "Everard's lost weight. He's ever so thin. I told him – you could do with some meat inside you!"

The good thing was that these flare-ups were quickly forgotten and everything returned to normal, with Larry just as friendly and just as funny next time you saw him. There didn't appear to be any bearing of grudges... unless, that is, you happened to be Wincey Willis...

It's important to put these incidents into perspective of course. I have spent a few pages talking about them, but only because they maybe revealed something about the real Larry Grayson at that time. I can't spend an equivalent number of pages talking about all the many hilarious, easy-going, happy times working with Larry, but trust me when I say that there really were a massive number of those. The hiccups were two brief incidents in the space of a hugely enjoyable nine month period of our dealings with Larry. And I suppose it's fair to say that if I hadn't happened to book Wincey, and if Alan Walsh hadn't wanted to use that tacky film clip, then we might have only ever seen the cheery, easy side of Larry Grayson. It may also be true that Larry was perhaps a little more touchy and susceptible to blowing a gasket at that time, as, unbeknown to us, it was a difficult period of his private life. My last word on all this is that I loved working with Larry, and the vast majority of the time he was funny, kind, warm and endearingly vulnerable. I am proud to have known him.

A Question of Entertainment appeared to be a successful and popular series. Critically it was well received, and all three of the stars were consistently funny. We had a faithful following of around five or six million viewers, which was a highly respectable rating, especially as we were scheduled against one of ITV's perennially popular Sunday night blockbuster dramas – I think it may have been *London's Burning.* However the BBC bosses in London decided that our series wasn't cutting edge enough, and they refused to recommission the show in its current form.

The truth is we had the right show at the wrong time. A couple of years earlier and it would have been warmly embraced by the BBC. Just a few years later and it would have been perceived as a major coup to gather so many iconic entertainment legends and national treasures together to have fun. However this was that lamentable period when all television executives were running scared about mainstream entertainers. I don't think it was anything to do with what the vast majority of TV viewers actually wanted, the senior figures in television were all just terrified of not appearing to be up to speed with current trends in comedy. There was also a tiresome growing obsession with every programme on TV having to appeal to a trendy youthful audience. I always felt this was a strange and quite unrealistic goal, as by far the largest percentage of people who watch TV on a regular basis are thirty-five-plus parents and grandparents, not trendy youngsters who, quite rightly, prefer to be out having fun. Middle-aged or older viewing audiences are rarely catered for, or even considered.

The BBC hierarchy seemed to like the idea of a celebrity showbiz quiz, but the brutal decision was made to revamp *A Question of Entertainment* completely. Even the title was changed – it became *That's Showbusiness.* Larry, Ken Dodd and Tom O'Connor were unceremoniously axed and replaced by new team captains Gloria Hunniford and Kenny Everett, with DJ Mike Smith in the chair. It didn't sound like terribly 'cutting edge' casting to me, but then I would say that wouldn't I? The guest team members inevitably came from the same celebrity pool that I had been tapping, so nothing much changed there, to be frank. It had also been decreed by the faceless ones at BBC television centre in London that not one single person who had been on the production team of *A Question Of Entertainment* was permitted to work on *That's Showbusiness.* I assume they were worried we might infect the new team with our filthy populist mainstream thinking. Fortunately I had been offered a job as an ITV producer, so I had something positive to move on to, but it must have been very galling for my friend Alan Walsh to have his baby snatched right from under his nose, and to sit and watch another producer move in to the next door office and take his show over.

Truthfully the new look, re-titled 'cutting edge' version wasn't really any different from the series we had made, other than its line-up of regulars, who weren't nearly as funny, even if they did have a slightly lower combined age. In the end a celebrity quiz about entertainment is just that. Take it or leave it. The interesting thing was that the new show wasn't any more successful than our series had been either. Their viewing figures struggled to match ours, so the new team and their three stars weren't asked to make another series, and they were all dropped just as brutally as we had all been.

It was a sign of the times though. Mainstream hit shows were being axed, and top performers, who had made an awful lot of money for the television companies don't forget, were now being shunned and reviled simply because they didn't comply to the new trendy but ruthless thinking in television.

Larry, Ken and Tom I think could all see the writing on the wall for their kind of entertainment on TV, so it must have been terribly hurtful for them to be dropped by the BBC like that, after so many years of loyal service making hit shows. They would all struggle, like all mainstream performers of that time, to find any more work on television, with all the jobs going to the new wave of aggressive, often politically-motivated young comics.

It was a particularly trying time for Larry. Not only had his hugely successful, but all-too-brief television career come to an end, but his dream of retiring to Torquay had backfired badly, and his circle of friends had pretty much deserted him. Even his live appearances were marred by Gay Lib protesters, and, let's face it, touring was hard work for a sixty-five-year-old man who had never enjoyed the best of health. Not only that but poor Fan's state of mind was getting worse and she needed a lot of looking after, so he couldn't be far from Nuneaton for too long. Fan had been Larry's rock ever since he was a baby, but now she was forgetful and no longer really understood what was going on around her. It was becoming increasingly apparent that it was now only a matter of time before she would have to be put into a care home. That must have been a heartbreaking realisation for Larry.

All those years of patiently waiting to become a star, then when it happened, it was short-lived because of changing fashions and a new enemy, misplaced political correctness. There is no doubt that a degree of political correctness was necessary after some of the racist, misogynist and homophobic excesses of the 1970s, but again babies and bath water spring to mind. Larry's style was suddenly passé, and the new television stars were either 'right-on' alternative comedians or rather bland presenters like Noel Edmonds, Phillip Schofield, Mike Smith, Sue Lawley and Gloria Hunniford.

In the same television period of 'mainstream cleansing' shows like *The Good Old Days* had been axed, so there weren't even guest appearances on that for Larry to look forward to any more. He actually gave an interview to a journalist on the subject, saying he thought the BBC had made a grave error by axing such a popular programme. It didn't make any difference though – the BBC were unmovable on such things.

A Question of Entertainment ended up being Larry's last television series. All that was left for him on the small screen after that was the occasional chat show, a guest appearance on Paul Daniels' BBC1 magic series, and the odd *Pebble Mill at One*, plus one timely last chance to take his final bow on a massive show...

16

... the final chapter... and friends to the end...

In 1988 Larry's close friend Arthur Marshall had a minor heart attack. He did recover from that, but another illness followed and he sadly died in January 1989. It was yet another blow for Larry. In a tragic irony the poodle which Larry had named after Arthur died around the same time. Larry bought another poodle puppy, a chocolate coloured one, which he called William, this time named after his friend Dora Bryan's son, but of course the real Arthur Marshall was irreplaceable. His death was to leave another major hole in Larry's life as, even when Larry moved back to Nuneaton, he and Arthur had phoned one another every weekend for a gossip and a giggle, and to reminisce about their favourite film stars.

Larry had started, for the first time in his life, to put on weight. It had a lot to do with the medication he was on, and of course his inactivity. He didn't much like it however, and was concerned about his image. Larry was worried that William, his pet poodle, was also putting on weight, so he rather underfed him, to keep him slim. He said he didn't want people making comments about that fat old comedian walking his fat dog. This enforced hunger made William understandably snappy, and he in fact bit Fan a couple of times, which upset Larry. Fan's dementia was getting worse and it was getting to the point where he couldn't cope without professional help. He found it difficult to understand what was happening to her, and it made him almost irritable with her on occasions, then he'd feel terribly guilty. It was a vicious circle.

Worse was to follow. By 1989 Larry could no longer handle Fan's needs and her frailties, and, extremely reluctantly, he had to have her put in a nursing home. The dementia had got to the point where she barely recognised him. It must have been heartbreaking for Larry. He tortured himself that it was his fault that she was ill, and he'd wrestled for a long time with the decision about the home. He'd get tearful with frustration, feeling a failure that he'd let Fan down after all she'd done for him.

Christmas 1990 was spent in snowy Austria with friends, but that ended disastrously. On New Year's Eve Larry was walking out for tea when he slipped on the icy pavement, fell headlong and cracked five ribs. He was rushed to hospital in Salzburg where the doctor strapped him up. Larry was in great pain and suffering from shock when the doctor returned with a glass of champagne in his hand and wished him, in broken English, a happy new year. It could only happen to Larry.

He felt scared and lonely in a foreign hospital where he couldn't speak the language and struggled to make himself understood. He pleaded to be discharged, but the doctor said he was in too delicate a state, and feared that pneumonia might set in if he tried to make his way home unassisted. The Salzburg hospital finally agreed to discharge him if he chartered a private plane with a nurse in attendance. This was an expensive option, but Larry was so desperate and so low in spirits that he readily agreed. The tiny plane would normally have frightened the life out of him, but he felt so ill he was just relieved to be heading home, and didn't care. They flew him to Coventry where a car was waiting to whisk him back to the safety and familiarity of Nuneaton. The trauma of this painful fall affected his eyesight, which led to two operations to put implants into his eyes. Larry loathed feeling so mortally vulnerable and so housebound, and he succumbed to a deep depression which went on for months. He didn't want to see anybody or do anything. There was no joy left in his life at all.

Towards the end of that awful year Paul Vaughan phoned Larry and cautiously asked him how he felt about doing another pantomime. Having been off the television for so long Larry's bankability had slipped dramatically, so it wasn't even a major prestigious theatre that had requested him. The Palace Theatre in Mansfield wanted him to play Wishee Washee in *Aladdin*, alongside Jean Rogers from *Emmerdale* and Mike Berry from *Are You Being Served?*, neither of them exactly big star names. Larry was really a bit old for the part of Aladdin's cheeky ne'er-do-well brother, and the short engagement was a bit of a comedown from the big lavish long-running pantos he'd headlined in all the major cities in his heyday. However the small

Nottinghamshire town of Mansfield was only an hour from Nuneaton, which meant a driver could get him home every night, so, with some reservations, he agreed. It was the best thing he could have done, as it turned out. The successful five week run, with a company he loved, was a very happy time and proved to be therapeutic, lifting him back out of his dark depression of 1991.

One of the true friends that did remain loyal and attentive during the last despondent lonely years was a local Nuneaton man called Tony Knight. Tony had been a shop steward, and was a concert secretary at one of the many working men's clubs where Larry performed regularly before television fame elevated him to the top of the bill in big theatres. Tony Knight went far enough back that he'd known and booked Larry when he was still appearing as Billy Breen. Over the years they had struck up an enduring friendship. He was a good friend to Larry long before the fair-weather spongers had arrived on the scene, and was still a good friend long after the spongers had disappeared again. Tony always called Larry 'Bill', which was something that only genuinely long-term friends and family did, and Larry was always interested in how Tony was doing with the union and down at his club. Politically they were at opposite ends of the spectrum, but real friendship transcends even the furthest extremes of politics.

A couple of old friends re-emerged when Larry needed company, and after Fan had been admitted to the nursing home. They were Barry Anthony and Ray Young, a gay couple from South Yorkshire who had been a song and dance act before turning their hands to designing glitzy stage costumes for the likes of Shirley Bassey. Larry had met them way back in the 1950s when they were performing together on the same bill, and had befriended them. They hadn't seen much of Larry in the famous years, but they were quick to offer their friendship when he needed it towards the end. In fact they were with Larry when he died.

Another close friend and confidante, who almost unofficially became Larry's personal psychotherapist, was a man called Thomas Bunn, 'Bunny' to his friends, and just plain 'Bunn' to Larry. Bunny is an openly gay man, who was in a very happy and contented long-term relationship with his live-in partner and companion, Dennis Docherty for thirty-six years, until Dennis's sad death in 2005. Thomas Bunn had trained for many years, first of all in psychiatric nursing and mental health, then in psychiatry itself, eventually becoming a lecturer on the subject, and a consultant in psychiatry.

I met up with Bunny, who was more than happy to talk to me about Larry as a friend, and also Larry's mental state in his final years. Larry never officially consulted him in a professional capacity, but he knew of Bunn's qualifications, and often confided in him in a way he didn't with other friends. In return Bunn would offer informed help and guidance as a friend, without it ever being on a formal patient / doctor basis. That all sounds terribly earnest, but actually Bunny has been a part-time comedy performer himself and has a great sense of humour, so he and Larry had a tremendous amount of fun and laughter together as well. There is no doubt however that Larry was leaning more and more on Bunn in his last years, because of his depressed state of mind.

They first met in 1972, backstage after a triumphantly riotous performance by Larry in *Aladdin* at The Hippodrome Theatre in Birmingham. "A masterclass in light camp innuendo and gesturing" as Bunny described it. Bunn simply wanted to introduce himself as a big fan, having watched and loved all of Larry's TV shows. His partner Dennis wasn't particularly interested in broad comedy theatre, so he was at home working. After a 'small gin' and a convivial chat in Larry's star dressing room the two men exchanged contacts and said goodbye. Bunn went home to tell Dennis all about this exciting meeting, never really expecting to hear from Larry again. Much to his surprise and delight, quite a few weeks later, with the panto now a fond but distant memory, Bunny got a phone call from Larry thanking him for coming to the theatre and for popping backstage to introduce himself, adding: "I did enjoy it duck!". They then chatted and giggled about everything and nothing for an eternity, beginning a close friendship which was to endure for over twenty years. As I have said before Larry could take to people very quickly, and then friendship was easy, because he was such good company, and so funny. Larry became particularly close to both Bunn and Dennis during the last ten years of his life, as his hectic work commitments eased and he had more time for true friends, and I suppose because he needed and valued genuine friendships more. During that period Larry moved back to Nuneaton, and Bunn and Dennis were living in Acocks Green near Birmingham, so they were not quite neighbours, but definitely close enough to be able to 'pop in'.

Fan was in no fit state to socialise and, according to both Bunny and Paul Vaughan, May's family didn't bother too much with Larry in his last few years, so he spent his last four Christmases with Bunn and Dennis, enjoying the relaxed normality, the safe secure privacy, and Dennis's home cooking. Bunny says towards the end Larry wasn't looking after himself properly, so, when ever Larry visited, Dennis would pack him off at the end of the day with a couple of plated meals covered in Clingfilm to go in the fridge and be reheated at a later date. The next day Bunny would always get a call: "Tell Dennis that meal he made up for me was the cow's ankle!", which was Larry's unsmutty way of describing something that is so good the rest of us would compare it with a couple of less seemly parts of a male dog's anatomy.

The depression had even got to a state where Larry wasn't always bothered if his clothes were clean, which was very surprising, and indeed worrying, when you remember what a fastidious and fussy child he'd been, and how he'd always prided himself in his immaculate appearance on stage. His motto, as an entertainer, had always been: "It's no crime to be poor, but it's unforgivable to look poor." It was almost as though he had finally lost the will to live.

Bunny said that, in his professional opinion, Larry suffered all his life from endogenous depression, which is genetic and inherent; as opposed to reactive depression, which is involuntarily self-inflicted through tragic or unhappy circumstances. This explains Larry's dramatic mood swings. Bunny said some days he'd be almost suicidal, then the next he'd forgotten all about that, and was his usual chirpy self again. Even though endogenous depression is hard-wired into the brain, it can still be affected and triggered by outside influences, so when Larry was busy, work was fun, and he was surrounded by friends, he could remain on a high, but when ever he wasn't working and was alone the dark cloud would come over him and he would sink into a depression. Obviously towards the end of his life there were more of these depressed lows because he was lonely and he no longer had the excitement and distraction of his beloved career. Not only that but there were more genuine tragedies in his life to drag him down. Endogenous depression is biochemical, so antidepressant medication might well have helped him, but Bunny said Larry was of that generation where you didn't go running off to the doctor when you were depressed, you just had to 'pull yourself together', which of course isn't always possible.

While I was with Bunny I asked him about Larry's sexuality and whether he felt Larry might have been envious of his and Dennis's successful and very happy long-term relationship. Like everybody else I have spoken to, Bunny said that Larry definitely wasn't a predatory promiscuous gay man. He believed that most of Larry's energies, which the vast majority of people channel into sexual relationships, was channelled into his career, and showbusiness, which was everything to him, and far more important than sex. Bunny didn't try to pretend that Larry was a saint, or even a monk, acknowledging that Larry could flirt outrageously with men or make admiring comments, especially after a gin and tonic, but he wasn't the sort to seek casual sexual liaisons.

As far as a cosy long-term relationship goes Bunny felt that Larry simply wasn't capable of that sort of commitment. For a start he was happy living with Fan. They had become very set in their ways, and prudish Fan wouldn't have approved of a man moving in with them anyway. However Bunny thinks the most significant factor was that Larry was too selfish in his ways, and wasn't capable of adapting his lifestyle to accommodate anybody else in his life on a permanent basis. He had carved out a life for himself and Fan which, whilst unusual, worked remarkably well for them, and he wasn't about to upset that fragile and important applecart. Bunny believes, as I do, and have said earlier in this book, that Larry was very comfortable in his own unique skin. He wasn't tortured with guilt about his sexuality like his contemporary, Kenneth Williams.

In 1994, less than a year before he died, Larry sent a long letter to Pauline Pearson, his fan and long time correspondent, which is unusually bitter about his beloved showbusiness and the direction it had taken. He was clearly feeling frustrated and angry during what was another desperately low period of his life:

"... I can't stick the so-called stars with all the filth and no talent. I had the best years, playing the best shows and the lovely theatres, now all gone, and worked with real stars and clever acts who didn't always top the bill. You don't see the like of them today I'm afraid..."

His tone then lightens, but you can tell he is just trying to put on a brave face and make things sound better than they actually are:

"... I am fit and very well and happy, now completely retired from showbiz, no more stage shows or TV. Paul Vaughan, my manager, gets lots of offers for me to do TV and shows, but NO MORE... whoopee!!!!"

Another true and loyal friend in the lonely years was his manager Paul Vaughan. The truth is there were occasional offers of work, but nothing that Larry wanted to do. Many of them would have been beneath him, and he didn't want to demean himself like that. He wanted the public to remember him as he was when he was still right at the top of his game. Paul therefore was making no commission worth speaking of from his client, but he still valued Larry as a friend, so he remained his manager, confidante and advisor right up to the end.

Larry would phone Paul in those barren years and say: "Oh you must come over duck, I've got so much to tell you. Come and visit and I'll give you all the gossip and the news!" When Paul drove over from Worcester, which he tried to do at least every couple of weeks, he would ask Larry what the big news was. Of course there wasn't any news at all – Larry was just lonely and desperate to see a friendly face. Paul said the rooms in the bungalow were always rearranged every time he visited. Larry was so bored he'd move all the furniture around all on his own, just for something to do. He would ask Paul what he thought of the new lay-out, but, no matter how much Paul enthused, it didn't stop Larry moving everything again the minute he had left.

He'd do the same thing with Bunny Thomas, phoning him in his office at work, saying that he must come over, again with the promise of great news and endless gossip. Bunny would try to explain that he had a job and couldn't just drop everything on a whim, but Larry would insist that it was very important. Bunny would then feel obliged to get in his car, leaving his secretary with strict instructions to page him if he was needed urgently, and drive to Nuneaton. Of course there was no great news and there wasn't anything important, but Larry was just desperate for company.

One other significant person in Larry's final years was 'Robert The Vicar'. He was a character often mentioned in the Larry Grayson act as a friend of Everard's. However, like most of Larry's odd on-stage invisible entourage, the comedy vicar character was based on somebody who really did exist. He was based on The Reverend Dr Rob Marshall, now known to millions as the voice of BBC Radio 4's "Thought For The Day", plus Radio 2's "Pause For Thought", and countless other broadcasts.

Rob first met Larry when he was at university studying theology, in the late 1970s, early 1980s. He was the editor of the in-house student newspaper, and there was a large lesbian and gay group of students who regularly contributed articles and stories. They persuaded Rob to interview Larry for the paper. This was around the time when gay pressure groups were wanting to challenge Larry, so he was about to decline the interview until

Rob mentioned that he was studying to go into the church. That intriguing bit of information was sufficient to earn Rob an invitation up to 'The Garlands' in Nuneaton to have tea.

Larry asked more questions than he answered. He was fascinated to know all about the church, and why Rob wanted to be a vicar. Cheekily he asked if it was just because he enjoyed dressing up. Suddenly it became like a confessional. Larry told Rob about his frequent conversations with clairvoyants, and said that he knew he shouldn't talk to such people. He (untruthfully) professed that he didn't real believe in 'all that stuff', and he wondered if God would forgive him for listening to them, when he got to Heaven. Rob said he genuinely seemed to feel guilty about consulting Madame Credo.

Larry kept in touch with Rob and supported him throughout his Church of England ordination process. Unfortunately Larry couldn't be at the actual ordination ceremony because he was recording a *Generation Game*, but he did get his driver to take him to Rob's humble working class home in Hull, a week later, for a celebration roast dinner with Rob and his family. His parents couldn't believe that a Rolls Royce was parked outside their small home, and the man they had watched the night before on television was sitting across the table from them, sharing their roast beef and Yorkshire pudding.

Over the years Larry and Rob visited many churches together. Rob told me that Larry was always fascinated by the theatricality of it all – the magnificent splendour of the buildings, the colourful religious garments, the music, the drama, the almost showman-like structure of church services, etc. He also took an interest in the church generally, getting to know about the seasons of the church and church procedures. A lot of his early childhood Sunday school teachings and memories came flooding back.

Larry hadn't really been a regular church-goer, however he had always been a believer. He once said in an interview: "I'm only here because God said so, but the only time I go to church is when I'm passing through a village or town, and I creep in on my own and sit there." He said he always asked God to bless Fan, and make his next audience like him, because he loved them, adding: "I think if you don't believe in God, you're lost."

When he and Rob visited churches and cathedrals together Larry would always want a few minutes to go off and sit on his own in quiet contemplation. Presumably he was remembering his mother Ethel, his foster parents Jim and Alice, and of course his friend Tom, who was killed in action during the war. Rob said Larry could sit for twenty minutes alone sometimes, just thinking.

They remained in touch, but, in the last lonely years, Larry phoned Rob every Thursday, partly for a chat, and partly to keep his peace with his maker. A lot of time was spent on the phone with Larry planning his own funeral. He told Rob he didn't want a lot of moaning and wailing – it was to be a happy celebration of his life. He wanted Rob to officiate at the ceremony, or his 'final curtain' as Larry called it. To Larry it was to be his last performance, insisting that Rob get his timing correct and push the button at just the right moment. In those last years Larry wanted to know from Rob what life and death was all about. Although Larry wasn't a conventional church-goer, Rob says he did definitely believe in a better after-life in Heaven, and so didn't fear death. Bunny Thomas confirms that, although Larry would frequently talk about death, he wasn't afraid of dying.

In the autumn of 1994 Larry's old friend and former road manager Kevin Bishop, now a senior entertainment executive at the BBC, phoned Larry up to see if he would like to make a surprise guest appearance on that year's *Royal Variety Performance*, which he was producing. Larry protested a little at first, saying he didn't really have an act any more. Kevin told him that the audience would be so pleased to see him that all he had to was walk on and say hello, so Larry agreed, albeit with some trepidation. Kevin travelled up to Nuneaton to talk to Larry and tried to get him to structure a five minute spot, but Larry was still resistant to planning and rehearsal, and didn't want to commit himself to a fixed structure. Although the finished spot went down very well Kevin felt it would have been even better if Larry had followed his advice and planned the spot properly.

Because he was a close friend Kevin knew Larry's ex-directory number and had made the initial phone contact direct, without going through Paul Vaughan, Larry's manager, which would have been normal protocol for a producer booking an artist. A few days later Larry mentioned to Paul about his forthcoming appearance on the Royal Variety show, and Paul at first thought that Larry was losing his marbles and was being delusional. Slowly he realised that the royal command was real. Paul was surprised, but delighted for his friend and client, and offered him a lift to The Dominion Theatre in Tottenham Court Road where the Royal show was being staged that year, in the presence of HRH Prince Charles, The Prince of Wales. Larry had already made arrangements with a young security guard from a local store who was going to drive him down to London.

As a 'surprise guest' Larry was not officially billed on the show, so he got a huge round of applause when he walked on dragging his trademark gold-painted bentwood chair behind him. He looked as immaculate as ever in a light grey suit, but he looked ill and tired, and was suddenly showing his age, his hair thinner and his face puffy. He got a huge roar of approval with his opening line: "They thought I was dead!". Larry then did a very funny five minutes. It was a nostalgic moment seeing the act again – and it was all there – the aches and pains, Slack Alice, the cheeky innuendoes, the high camp asides, and he ended the spot with an emotional quaver in his voice as he said the words: "And before I go, for all you people at home, I must just say it once... Shut that door!" He got a huge ovation from the audience and the orchestra played him off to the familiar strains of his signature tune, Judy Garland's classic song "The Man That Got Away". He looked clearly moved by the reaction in the theatre, but then was furious with himself, because, in all his excitement at appearing on stage again in such a big show, he had completely forgotten to bow to Prince Charles, up in the Royal Box.

It was to be Larry's last ever appearance on television. Within two months he was dead. It seems rather appropriate, and a peculiar bit of showbiz kismet that his final words to his adoring public were "Shut that door".

On YouTube I have seen one edited clip of Larry on that Royal show where he appears to do very little. He walks on and says: "They thought I was dead!", then it cuts straight to the bit where he says his famous catchphrase. It seems rather sad and pathetic in that edited form, but, if you have only seen that cut-down version, don't be fooled. Elsewhere on YouTube there is the whole five minute spot, which is a great reminder of what an accomplished comedian he was, and how he artfully took the audience into his own hilarious little world.

The show aired in late November, and that Christmas Larry was in pain and suffering in silence, so as not to trouble anybody, or spoil the festive period. Lonely, with no career, and Fan in a care home, barely recognising him when he visited, he really felt he had nothing left to live for. His interest in all things other-worldly, in particular Red Indian spirit guides, rose to the fore during this painful period, and he would heartbreakingly say to Paul Vaughan: "They're ready for me. The spirit guides are preparing to take me away. It won't be long now...". Paul would try to buoy his spirits, but nothing really helped.

Larry spent that last Christmas with Thomas 'Bunny' Bunn and Dennis in Acocks Green, as he had done the previous three years. He teased Bunny by saying, in the preceding weeks, that he'd had other more attractive invitations, but the truth was he never really intended to see anybody else, and what was left of his 'family' hadn't even invited him. Bunny says he wasn't aware that Larry was particularly ill, although he did need a nap after his lunch, and he didn't stay too late. However he managed to eat a good meal, have some fun and stand for The Queen's Speech, as per tradition.

Larry had never been a fan of New Year's Eve, and had of course had that disastrous fall on the ice and snow in Austria on December 31st 1990, so it was a cruel irony that he collapsed and was rushed into hospital on New Year's Eve 1994 with a ruptured appendix. Paul Vaughan thinks he must have been in pain for quite some time, but Larry left it until it became critical before he did anything about it. An emergency operation was performed, and he was sent home several days later. Paul says Larry looked terrible, and not really fit to be discharged, but the hospital had said they needed the bed. Unbeknown to the nursing staff the acute peptic ulcers he'd suffered in previous years had flared up again, compounding the appendix problem. He was haemorrhaging badly and, no sooner had he got home, than doctors had to be called out once again. With Larry literally looking like death, they said they wanted to readmit him to hospital, but he pleaded not to be sent back. He'd had enough. Larry said he just wanted to stay in his own bed, surrounded by a handful of close friends and family. He slipped away peacefully during the night and was pronounced dead on January 7th 1995. He was just seventy-one.

Larry had given specific instructions in his will, using quite flowery language, about the funeral and Rob Marshall's involvement, so Paul Vaughan had to phone 'Robert The Vicar' and tell him that sadly his big moment had arrived. Rob was so shocked and upset he couldn't think straight at first, but then started planning an appropriate and fitting ceremony, which would comply to all of Larry's instructions and requests. First and foremost it was going to be a traditional Christian service, but Rob was keen to give a definite nod to Larry the entertainer, and Larry the son of Nuneaton and local hero. It was quite an ordeal for a young vicar because he was determined to do the whole thing without a script or notes in front of him, in front of a massive congregation, including many celebrities, not to mention TV news cameras.

It was the biggest funeral Nuneaton had ever seen. The odd bigoted civic dignitary might not have been so proud of the town's most famous son, but the real people of Nuneaton clearly loved Larry Grayson, and were going to miss him. The streets were lined with people as the coffin went slowly by, and Larry's local church, The Abbey Church of St Mary The Virgin in Nuneaton, was filled to overflowing. A huge number of acquaintances, friends and fans packed the churchyard outside to pay their respects and listen to the words of The Reverend Dr Rob Marshall through loudspeakers. They also heard the familiar voice of Dora Bryan as she read the lesson. This was not only a man who had put Nuneaton on the map, but also a man who had been a popular and much-loved neighbour, as well as a respected citizen. The wake, for close friends and family only, was held at The Chase Hotel in Higham Lane.

Sadly the only person who wasn't there was Fan. The dementia was so bad by this point that she simply didn't understand that Larry had died. There was no point adding to her confusion and taking her to a bustling funeral that wouldn't have meant anything to her, and would have been bewildering and possibly frightening. She never did really grasp that Larry was gone. Occasionally, in the following months, she would look round and ask visitors: "Where's Bill?", but she couldn't, or wouldn't, comprehend the sensitively phrased answer. Fan died in 1996, outliving her little Billy by over a year. She was eighty-seven.

There was a small private committal ceremony, after Larry's funeral, with a handful of his friends and family at the graveside in Oaston Road Cemetery in Nuneaton. It was a Hammond / White family grave, and a black marble headstone marks the spot to this day. Strangely the stone bears the odd mistake. Not least the birth year of Alice Hammond, Larry's foster mother. It confused me no end, until I saw her birth records, because it makes her out to have been twenty years older than her husband Jim, which of course was not the case.

A few months after Larry's death, on July 7th 1995 in fact, there was a memorial service held in central London at St Paul's Church in Covent Garden, often referred to as "The Actors' Church". This was more for his showbusiness friends and colleagues. I was pleased and proud to be invited to that myself, as the place was packed to the rafters with so many people wishing to pay their last respects. I did have a seat, but there were many people standing at the back of the large church that has seen tributes to so many of our showbiz and theatrical legends.

Obviously it was a sad occasion, but it was also a joyous celebration of a very funny man. Fittingly it was very showbizzy. The comedy actor Alfred Marks read a touching poem, and there were two hilarious eulogies from Larry's friends Terry Wogan and comedian Roy Hudd who made us all laugh with fond memories of Larry. We were even played into the church to an organ medley from *The Wizard of Oz*, one of Larry's favourite Judy Garland films. The most moving moment came when The Cannock Chase Orpheus Male Voice Choir sang the sentimental ballad "Take Me Home". The burly colliery choir filled the gallery of The Actors' Church, and raised the roof with their voices, leaving not a dry eye in the house. Soho impresario Paul Raymond, who had come from his own sick-bed to be there, said he was particularly moved by that moment. Paul Vaughan's choice of a Midlands colliery choir was of course a fitting tribute to Larry's foster father, coal miner Jim Hammond.

It seems to me that Larry lived a predominantly happy life, with some incredible highs, dogged by occasional darkly depressing lows. He enjoyed every minute of his showbusiness apprenticeship, and he really loved his stardom when it eventually came. The good thing was he probably appreciated it more, and was more grateful for the fame and the rewards than a younger comedian, because he was mature in years and in mind, and had struggled for so long. He never took anything for granted. Larry loved his audiences, and had a genuine love for people generally. He had many close friends and people who loved him and looked out for him. I have watched and read a huge number of interviews with Larry in the course of the research for this book, and what stands out every time is the sincerity with which he says what a wonderful life he had, and how he never felt bitter or angry in his younger struggling days when fame and fortune seemed so elusive.

Larry once said in an interview: "My needs are very simple really. I love to be home, I love a big coal fire, I love to watch television. A good laugh and I'm happy." To him there was nothing better than laughing with friends, something which happened often, and of course he returned the gift of laughter in spades.

In the same contemplative interview, given in his autumn years, he said: "I've had a wonderful life really – the theatre, and all the travelling. I've seen all the country, historic buildings, the seaside. I've met wonderful people – and been paid for doing it."

Yes there were dark times, and possibly it is a shame that he never found a life partner, but I think Larry Grayson wouldn't want anybody's pity, because he had an exciting and fulfilling life in a business he adored, surrounded by love and laughter. I'm sure he felt that was about as good as it gets. I don't think that anybody can say that everything has always been perfect and every moment of their life has been joyously happy – certainly nobody I know.

One thing that must not be forgotten, despite the depression and loneliness of his last few years, Billy Breen / Larry Grayson was a consummate and very clever entertainer. It struck me that in all the stories about his career, and all the reviews I have read, he always went down well where ever he appeared. I don't think I have seen one bad, or even mediocre critique. In fact his reviews are nearly all rave reviews. Of course, like any comedian, there must have been tricky audiences and tough nights, but generally he seems to have gone down a storm where ever he went, and in what ever environment. He may not have been a versatile all-round entertainer, but he was certainly adaptable. He was like a stand-up chameleon. He could adapt his unique style so seamlessly and so instinctively that audiences and critics loved him in just about every entertainment situation imaginable – working men's clubs, family seaside shows, major theatres, village halls, pantomimes, gay transvestite revues, seedy Soho pick-up joints, sophisticated nightclubs, The London Palladium and television. I would find it hard to think of any other comedian who has been feted in such a wide variety of environments. I'm sure that's how William Sully White would like to be remembered – as Larry Grayson, one of the funniest, beloved, most gifted and highly adaptable comedians of the late twentieth century.

The Last Word on the Man That Got Away

It has been a real labour of love to piece together Larry Grayson's previously never-told story, and it has been a great privilege and a pleasure to talk to so many people who knew him, admired him and worked with him, sharing our experiences and memories of a dear and funny man.

There are two attributes of Larry that have been mentioned time and time again by every single person that I have spoken to about him. Firstly that he was hilariously funny, off-stage as well as on; and secondly that he was immensely likeable, kind and warm as a human being. Praise for a comedian really doesn't get much better than that, does it? As somebody who was privileged to get to know him briefly myself I can't argue with either of those sentiments.

Larry used to end every show with these five genuinely sincere and emotional words to his audience: "I love you very much". Well I do hope you realised that we loved you too Larry... very much...